'A stark account of a talented police officer's breakdown...
This is a startli͏ book an͏ the final two chapters

'I read *Blue* more or less in one sitting. I thought it was
wonderful – very powerful, deeply moving and utterly
honest'

Henry Marsh, bestselling author of *Do No Harm* and
Admissions

'An honest look at the vulnerability that comes with bravery'
the i newspaper

'The effect of this honesty is to leave us both more appre-
ciative of police officers and more concerned for their well-
being, as well as encouraged that such a compassionate man
was promoted so vertiginously. He describes police work as
"fulfilling, humbling, inspiring, daunting, shattering, rewarding and soul-stirring" which is also a fair description of his
book'   Josh Raymond, *Times Literary Supplement*

'*Blue* is a remarkable, revealing and inspiring insight into
the worlds of the police and the policed. The stories told
are by turns heart-warming and saddening, moving and
maddening – it is an account of the very best and the very
worst of our society. It is a book which should be required

reading for all who aspire to public office, in any sector and at every level'

John Nichol, bestselling author of *Tornado Down*

'Brave and very honest'   Bear Grylls

'Admirably honest and movingly human... Sutherland asks us to look behind the faceless blue and see the individual people – "human and humane"... the everyday heroes and heroines who police our streets'   P.F. King, *The Spectator*

'A superb book by a superb police officer'

Charles Cumming

'This is a remarkable book: a diary which became a magnum opus on belief and success, on depression and despair. It is well written and intellectually demanding, profound and deeply moving. In places, it is funny; everywhere, it is thoughtful. It has as much to tell us about mental illness as it does about policing. And there is much love in it: for friends, for family, for life'   Alastair Stewart

'A fascinating, powerful and beautifully written insight into the life of a police officer'

Dan Walker, journalist and broadcaster

'It is rare for an officer to reveal such deep, personal experiences about the effect policing has had on his life as does John Sutherland. His memoir will expand people's understanding of what it means to be a police officer in Britain today, revealing the truth about the toll that a career in policing can have on those tasked with the responsibility of tackling crime. This is a brave and compelling account of policing from a very senior officer in the most renowned police force in the world'

Colin Taylor, author of *Life of a Scilly Sergeant*

'A gripping book... moving and really powerful... I highly recommend it'   Jumoke Fashola, BBC London

'Courageous and moving'
Tom Harper, *Sunday Times* Home Affairs Correspondent

'A bravely honest account of how confronting crime and its fallout took one police officer to breaking point. Thought-provoking and a reminder that there is no one looking after the people looking after us'

Steve Myall, *Daily Mail* Deputy Features Editor

'The book is both a love letter to policing and a very human account of John's collapse and recovery. It contains one of the best descriptions of living with depression which I have ever come across'   Sarah Meyrick, *Church Times*

'John's kindness, warmth and humanity shine through. I found *Blue* deeply inspiring'
Dr Tim Cantopher, author of *The Curse of the Strong*

John Sutherland is a father of three who lives with his wife and children in south London. For more than twenty-five years, he served as a Metropolitan Police Officer. He won the Baton of Honour as the outstanding recruit in his training-school intake and rose through the ranks to become a highly respected senior officer.

Over the course of his career, in which he was awarded several commendations, he worked in seven different London boroughs, in a variety of ranks and roles, and he was also posted to Scotland Yard on three separate occasions. His final operational job was as the Borough Commander of Southwark. John can be found on Twitter and Wordpress as 'policecommander'. *Blue* is his first book.

Blue

A Memoir

Keeping the Peace
and Falling to Pieces

John Sutherland

WEIDENFELD & NICOLSON

First published in Great Britain in 2017
This paperback edition first published in 2018 by Weidenfeld & Nicolson
an imprint of The Orion Publishing Group Ltd
Carmelite House, 50 Victoria Embankment
London EC4Y ODZ

An Hachette UK Company

1 3 5 7 9 10 8 6 4 2

A CIP catalogue record for this book is
available from the British Library.

ISBN 978 1 4746 0606 6

Typeset at The Spartan Press Ltd,
Lymington, Hants

Printed and bound by CPI Group (UK) Ltd,
Croydon, CRO 4YY

www.orionbooks.co.uk

For Bear

Contents

Locard's Principle:

'Every contact leaves a trace'

I. *Introduction*

Springtime in London, this remarkable, kaleidoscopic carousel of a city that is my home. This is where I've lived since I was a teenager, where my wife and I have chosen to raise a family – and where I've worked as a police officer for the last twenty years and more. Two working decades of the grandest of adventures, the finest of friendships and the deepest of sorrows.

Down the years, I've been posted all over London – seven different boroughs in a variety of roles and ranks, three separate stints at Scotland Yard, a mix of uniform and detective experience, north and south of the river – and my geography of the capital is defined as much by the scenes of incidents and crimes as it is by any more conventional set of landmarks or a map of the Underground. You could walk with me for miles and I could point out the block of flats where the murder took place, the street corner where I was assaulted, the stretch of road where the fatal crash happened, the place where I was sitting when I heard the shots fired, the silent memorial where my colleague fell. These things stay with you.

But I love what I do. Each day of my working life, I have had the opportunity and the responsibility to make a difference – sometimes all the difference in the world. It is my duty and my joy.

*

I am six months into my time as Borough Commander at Southwark, given charge of one of the more complex and demanding parts of town. It's the best job I've ever had, and I've had some really, really good ones. I'm surrounded by a brilliant, passionate and committed team and I'm facing a professional challenge of a different order to any that I've encountered before. This is the real thing and all that I've seen and experienced and learned since the day I took the oath has been in preparation for now.

At least, that's how it had seemed to be.

*

I've been feeling unwell for a couple of months and I'm getting steadily worse. I can't remember the last time I didn't feel shattered. Up to now, I've been putting the exhaustion down to the combination of a properly serious job, the delights and demands of a young family and the flat-out pace of London living. It's just how things are at this point in my life.

But that doesn't explain some of the other things I've begun to experience. I'm getting increasingly anxious and I don't know why. I've started waking in the middle of the night in a state of complete panic and I can't offer any reason to explain it. And I've started to feel desperately low: the seemingly unstoppable advance of the black dog of depression.

I have absolutely no clue what's happening to me and no idea how to respond. I am the climber who has lost his grip, now slipping and sliding towards the edge of the precipice. I am Canute facing a tide that will become a tsunami.

In the last decade, I've missed only five days' work through sickness. I take pride in my attendance record. Like a significant number of my colleagues, I just don't 'do' sick and I'm wary, suspicious even, of many of those who do. So I just keep going, defiantly trying to push forwards in the face of something that is, increasingly and unrelentingly, stronger than me. Like a rugby player in the front row of a losing scrum, I'm struggling to hold my ground. That sense of duty, that overwhelming feeling of responsibility, a thousand officers and staff to lead, a community of tens of thousands to protect, any number of eye-watering operational challenges, guns and knives and drugs and homicidal maniacs, a family to provide for.

And it all just keeps coming.

*

Last Thursday of April. I walk into the control room on the ground floor of Southwark Police Station, to oversee the afternoon's operational briefing. The room is laid out like a lo-fi (and low-budget) version of the deck of the *Starship Enterprise*: banks of computer terminals, swivel chairs, flickering CCTV monitors, ringing phones and crackling radios – and a sense of unexpected possibilities.

One of the PCs looks up from his screen and chirps in my direction: 'Guv'nor, it looks like we've just had a murder...'

From the tone and inflection of his voice, he might just as well have been reading the football scores. There are no more details at this stage, but that single sentence already feels like more than I can cope with.

I couldn't tell you how many murders I've dealt with down the years – how many dead bodies I've seen; how many traumatic cases I've come across. And I've always been able to take things in my stride. It just goes with the territory. But now I'm stumbling. The thought of another life taken, another blood-soaked scene and another shattered family is just too much to bear. I make it through to the end of the meeting and back to my office up on the first floor. I break a habit and close the door. I don't think anyone noticed, but I'm only just holding it together.

I slump into a chair. Get a grip, man. The phone rings. It's the PC from the control room again: 'Good news, Boss – we haven't had a murder...' He pauses: 'But we have just had someone jump off one of the bridges into the Thames.'

I put the phone down, return to my seat and, for the first time in my working life, the thought occupies the whole of my mind: *I don't know if I can do this any more.*

II. *B.C. – Before Coppering*

The truth is, I was never going to make it as a shoplifter.

I'm fourteen years old and I live in Basingstoke – a place known as 'Donut City' to local CB Radio users, on account of the absurd number of roundabouts in and around town. Actually, the roundabouts are one of the more exciting features of the local area. I live with my family – Mum, Dad and two younger sisters – on a quiet residential street in a housing development at the edge of town. It's a friendly enough place, but nothing ever happens here.

I have braces on my teeth, a terrible haircut and a pair of ears that seem to belong to a bigger head.

It's a clear summer day and I'm at the top end of the town centre, riding my mum's bike. It's a classic early eighties ladies' design: no top tube and a tasteful wicker basket attached to the front handlebars. It is, without question, the worst getaway vehicle of all time.

I've got a bit of previous for nicking stuff from shops: mostly top-shelf magazines and assorted confectionery. I'm

5

not quite sure how it started and even less sure how I haven't been caught. I'd have spotted me a mile off.

The truth is, I'm boring – homework always handed in on time, polite to a fault, not normally brave enough to step out of line. But shoplifting has become something of a habit, not least motivated by the desire to impress one of the older boys in the year above me at school. Today it's just me, though, and my target is the newsagent's along from the town hall. I'm after a packet of scampi-flavoured fries – the sort Dad sometimes buys in the pub.

I lean Mum's bike up against the wall and venture through the shop door, attempting anonymity and looking guilty as hell. The shop assistant is looking the other way.

Grab and go. Back out onto the street.

I haven't even made it to my miserable set of wheels when I feel a firm adult hand on my right shoulder. I almost pass out with fright, quite possibly the closest I've ever been to soiling myself. The hand in question belongs to some interfering grown-up who is more vigilant that your average newsagent. He has witnessed my felony and marches me back into the shop.

I am a stammering, stuttering impression of myself, absolutely terrified. *I'm going to be arrested. I'm going to be expelled. I'm going to be sent to live in the garden shed.*

None of these things happens. In fact, the man behind the counter just looks at me with an air of weary resignation, takes the packet and gestures at me to leave.

I mumble an apology and promise never to do it again. I mean it.

*

In March 1970, I'm the first new addition to my family. I'm born to a grieving mother (her old man died, far too soon, while I was on the way) and an ailing father. Dad is a Church of England priest suffering with bipolar. A wonderful man with a hateful condition. And he's been battling it for years. Mum is a teacher and the long-suffering other half of an enormously challenging relationship. In its way, Dad's mental illness has had as much of an impact on her as it has on him. And she's been battling it for years. Two good people stumbling their way through the deep valleys and steep climbs that life throws their way.

And then me.

Over the years, home will be a bittersweet thing: frequently confusing, occasionally violent, ultimately heartbreaking. Mum and Dad will love the best they can. But life hurts.

*

In 1972, my baby sister Annie is born. Three years later, we're on a family break, staying with folk who live on the South Coast. Our host is a doctor and, not to put too fine a point on it, he saves my sister's life. He notices that something's out of place with her right eye and tells Mum and Dad to get her checked out properly as soon as we get home. The advice is heeded, Annie is diagnosed with cancer of the retina and surgeons have no option but to remove the eye.

I find myself walking down long white corridors at Bart's Hospital in London, a five-year-old boy in a suddenly serious and grown-up world, trying to reassure his mum that everything is going to be all right. Hard to measure or understand the impact of those days on me – all attention, quite under-standably, is on my little sister. Apparently, though, I'm learn-ing that my part in life is to make sure everyone else is OK.

With Annie in hospital, we stay in an unfamiliar London flat with people who are strangers to me. While we're there, they get burgled and I watch, fascinated, as a forensics officer dusts for prints.

Annie survives and flourishes. I tumble along.

*

I don't know how they came to be there, but the police are parked on the drive outside, paying a friendly visit to the vicarage. They're driving one of those specially equipped and modified motorway Range Rovers and, much to my delight, I get to clamber all over it. I watch, spellbound, as the mechanism housing the blue light on the roof of the car spirals several feet into the air. A small seed is planted.

*

Later the same year, one sister becomes two. Her name is Mary. No life-threatening illnesses this time, just a little bundle of apparently untroubled life. And our family is complete – aside from a succession of cats that get run over and dogs that don't.

It is a religious upbringing, lived in a collection of church settings where the certainty of what people stand against can seem much clearer than the knowledge of what they stand for. Most people will mean well most of the time, but that doesn't help. I am left in possession of a seemingly endless set of rules and haunted by a crippling sense of guilt – the inescapable feeling of never quite being good enough.

*

The happiest times of my earlier years are with my best friend, Titus. He lives in the village next door. He's born ten days after me and we're thrown together from the very beginning. His dad was a Motor Torpedo Boat Commander during the Second World War and he re-enacts naval battles for us on the kitchen table, using cutlery and assorted condiment jars as the craft in his tales. He later did well in the City and they have a large and wonderful home.

Endless hours and days spent outdoors – climbing trees, making camps, racing go-karts, scrambling through woods and fields, inhabiting tales in which we are the heroes – coming in to raid the fridge, before setting out again. These are the things I remember more clearly.

*

In 1977, we move from village to town and I become the boy from Basingstoke. The place with all the roundabouts. When I'm not running around outside with footballs and friends, I lose myself in books, captivated by the alchemy of storytelling. Narnia stays longest in my memory, as a place of adventure and wonder, of dryads and fauns, giants and centaurs, of Aslan and the triumph of good over evil. I let my imagination run free.

*

For most of my childhood, I am completely oblivious to Dad's illness – certainly at any conscious level. He was into amateur dramatics in his student days and he puts on enough of a show to leave me none the wiser. All I know is that he's my dad: the man who spends countless hours kicking footballs with me, the person who wrestles with me as I test my strength against his and the one who plays goodness knows how many rounds of my favourite Battle of Britain board game. When I pick up some horrible virus and begin to hallucinate all manner of fearful things, he reassures me and lets me share his bed. He's my hero. Which is exactly what a father should be to his son.

One afternoon, he borrows an old Fiat 500 from a friend and takes me out for a spin. We're still living in the sepia days before the interfering twins, Health and Safety, have ruined the potential for childhood tomfoolery and Dad is gloriously relaxed about these things. The car's canvas sunroof is pulled all the way back and I am allowed to stand, unrestrained, on the front passenger seat with my head poking out – a small papal imitation touring the roads that surround the town centre. We are spotted by the local Old Bill and get pulled over. Dad is given a ticking off, but they're friendly enough and leave it at that.

*

Every summer, we make a family pilgrimage to the wonderful Pembrokeshire coastline in South Wales. It's a place of happiness: of rockpools and waves, clifftops and caves, puffins and gannets and boat rides and Freddie, the old dog who lives at the St Brides Hotel and chases the tyres of the cars that go by.

I am about ten years old. On another lazy, sun-bathed afternoon, the Little Haven lifeboat is launched and word goes round the beach that someone has fallen from the cliffs not far away. I latch on to the rumours, put my fishing net to one side and scan the sea for the return of the crew. As they wheel the rib back up the beach, I'm drawn close enough to see the canvas body bag resting inside. I'm completely fascinated.

*

I'm in my last year at the local junior school. One afternoon, when lessons are done for the day, I'm walking home and fiddling innocently with a plastic spoon I've picked up some-where along the way. PC Ferguson ('Fergie' to his unadmir-ing public) is the local community police officer. He's passing by in the opposite direction and, for reasons known only to him, decides that it's my turn for a rollicking. He stops me, accuses me of using the spoon to flick stones at passing cars and gives me a right earful. I'll happily confess to any of my past crimes, but Fergie could not be more wrong. I'm doing nothing of the sort and he succeeds only in scaring the living daylights out of me. I arrive home in tears and Dad makes a complaint to the local police station. A day or two later, Fergie turns up at our front door to apologise. Bet he enjoyed doing that.

*

It's March 1984 and I'm riding my bike home from school. It's Annie's birthday and Mum has asked me to pick up some stuff from the shops on the way. I'm heading along Hackwood Road past the War Memorial Park, when I signal to turn right into Cliddesden Road. Perhaps surprisingly for a fourteen-year-old, I'm a reasonably sensible cyclist and I do everything as I should. But the driver waiting to pull out from Cliddesden Road just doesn't see me. As I am halfway through my turn, he dabs the accelerator and slams straight into me. I hit the road hard but, by some miracle, avoid hitting my head. Not many kids are wearing cycle helmets in the early eighties and it could so easily have been game over.

The main damage is to my left knee, which gets jammed between bike frame and tarmac. Assorted motorists get out of their cars and help me to the side of the road. I'm crying and in shock, but all I can think about is my sister's big day and the errand Mum has asked me to run. I try to reassure everyone that I'm OK and insist that I want to make my own way home. The concerned strangers should have taken the decision out of my hands. They should have called the police and an ambulance. They should have looked after me. But I must have been pretty damn determined.

Left alone, I limp the mile or so to the local shops near our house, pulling my broken bike alongside me. My knee is killing me but, compelled by some misplaced sense of duty, I'm absolutely set on doing what's been asked and expected of me. I buy the things on Mum's list and cover the last quarter of a mile to our back door. The tears are flowing freely now.

Dad scoops me up and drives me to A&E. He helps me through the automatic doors at the hospital and in for an X-ray. The verdict is that nothing is broken, just very heavy bruising. I miss the birthday celebrations at home.

*

In the summer of 1985, we move to London. Dad has a new job working with a church not far from Buckingham Palace. It doesn't pay much, but there's an amazing London townhouse to go with the role and I'm allowed to have the big bedroom on the top floor. But I'm only halfway through my O-Levels, so Mum and Dad decide that I should stay with friends in Basingstoke in order to get my grades. It means a weekly commute between Hampshire and the capital and, for nine long months, I never quite belong in either place.

I am confused by adolescence and have no one to walk and talk me through the mysteries of it all. I guess Mum and Dad have enough to contend with.

I still don't understand Dad's illness – what it is or what it means. While I'm stuck in Basingstoke, he has a severe manic episode and is admitted to the Maudsley Hospital.

My Headmaster, a good man, pulls me into his office and tells me that he knows I'm having a tough time. He wants to know if there's anything he can do to help. While I appreciate his kindness, I genuinely have no idea what he's talking about. Somehow, his words don't connect or make sense. I mean, I know that Dad is sick. But that's all I know. The rest is just a mystery.

I wander into the town centre and spend some of my pocket money on a couple of books I think Dad will like – a collection of Garfield cartoons and the latest James Bond novel. I pack them into a padded envelope with a handwritten note and send them up to London. I want to make things OK for him.

One weekend, Mum takes me to visit him and I find myself walking with her down another hospital corridor, white-walled and pictureless, on the way to his simple, cell-like room. We take him out for lunch at the old Harvester restaurant in Dulwich. I don't remember the conversation and I don't know what – or how – to feel. It's just grim and I'm lost.

*

It's 1987, I'm seventeen years old and I'm standing on Hammersmith Broadway, waiting for the bus to school. I live permanently in London now: the finest city in the world. I have spots. I hate having spots, particularly the large, vivid one that forms on the tip of my nose, announcing my arrival wherever I go.

I'm now a sixth-form pupil at St Paul's School in west London. This unexpected turn of events rounds out a gloriously mongrel education, one that has taken in village primary, prep school paid for by Titus's dad, Basingstoke Comp, church-run secondary and now, reputedly, one of the finest public schools in the land.

I'm not quite the right shape for the place. I've never been taught how to play rugby and I've never sat my backside in a rowing eight, but I'm about to get a better education than I bargained for. I've landed something called a 'state-assisted place'. I'm not entirely sure what that is or how I got it, but it means that the bill sent to Mum and Dad at the end of my first term is £13.99 – to cover the purchase of a badminton racquet. I have no idea how fortunate I am.

But, on a grey west London morning, I'm hardly enthused by the prospect of another school day. Sitting in classrooms has never been my thing. As the minutes meander and the number 33 fails to appear, I catch sight of a policeman walking down the opposite side of the road: a uniform going nowhere in particular. Knowing what I know now, he was probably bored, tired, cold and hungry. But none of that crosses my mind as I find myself momentarily transfixed. *That's what I want to do.* Something inside me just clicks. It's an almost physical sensation and from then on I never seriously consider doing anything else.

*

What on earth makes someone want to join the police? All sorts of reasons, of course. Most coppers will simply tell you that they want to make a difference – and they will be telling you the truth.

As a confused and confusing teenager, I'm not sure this is my first thought. More than anything else, at this moment in time, I envy the fact that the man in uniform passing by on the other side of the road isn't facing the immediate prospect of double History with Mr Dean. But the idea begins to grow. There's something about the sense of adventure, the *Boy's Own* thrill of it all. Then there's the realisation that I won't have to sit behind a desk in some soulless office space, and that no two days are ever likely to be the same. The chances are that I will be tested to my very limits. Perhaps beyond. It's so much more than a nine to five. And it's so much more than just another way to make ends meet. It's a vocation – a calling, even. Police officers refer to it as 'The Job'.

*

Still seventeen and I'm just back from a summer music festival. The best of times. It's a beautiful August day. Mum meets me at the door of the house. She walks me straight out onto the first-floor roof terrace and tells me that Dad has gone. Left us. Just like that. And in that single, stunned moment, my world falls apart. He is the great landmark of my life, the one from whom I take all my bearings. Without him, I will be hopelessly lost. I climb the stairs to my room on the top floor and sit on the edge of the bed with my head in my hands. I am punch drunk and weeping. Absolutely nothing makes sense but, in the days and weeks to come, the realisation will emerge that I'm the man of the house now.

I just didn't see it coming, despite the fact that the signs were there. There were Dad's deepening mood, unexpected obsessions and sometimes erratic behaviour. Then there was Mum's unhappiness. A good woman in an absolutely impossible situation. She and my sisters had spent that summer out of London, staying in a friend's cottage. They were escaping, but that fact had somehow passed me by. I stayed in town, living on the adrenalin of my latter teens and surrounded by friends. Dad was at home and was seriously ill. But my head was elsewhere and my defences were firmly in place. The signs were there, I just couldn't read them.

Home will become a less familiar place to me. Mum is remarkable, but Dad is gone.

*

He retreats to a monastery down in Dorset and, for six months, we don't see or hear from him. Life carries on until, as the eldest, it falls to me to go and see him first. I'm caught between fear and longing.

I travel down by train for a bewildered reunion. I'm numb with pain, speechless with questions and utterly adrift in my sadness. He has become, in many ways, a stranger to me.

There is so much about him that I don't know and even more that I can't begin to understand. But loving him is unavoidable. And unavoidably painful. In many of the years ahead, I will be more of a dad to him than he is able to be to me.

I spend the night sleeping fitfully on the floor beside his bed. The following day, he drops me back at the station and we mumble our goodbyes. There's a small green can of Heineken sitting on the dashboard of the car he's borrowed. Something to dull his senses a little.

I make my way to the deserted far end of the platform, getting as far as I can from my fellow travellers, and quietly disintegrate. As I exhale deeply, a silent, primal scream escapes: the unheard accompaniment to a fracturing of my soul. It is far worse than anything I felt on the day he first left. And there will be endless excruciating goodbyes down the years.

*

Mum and Dad divorce the next year, just as I'm preparing for my A-Levels. I learn to cope. Just me, Mum and my sisters. Be strong now.

We have to give up the house that went with Dad's job and home for the next year or two becomes a couple of rooms upstairs with the local vicar and his wonderful family. I share with Mum – the awkwardness of teenage years compounded. Mum snores.

*

In March 1988, I turn eighteen. I'm in possession of a provisional driving licence, which I use to verify my age. One evening I head out with Alan, a friend from school, to a pub on the Kings Road. I take my ID just in case, but the bar staff don't appear too bothered about who they serve. And we drink beer like men.

As we roll back home later on, I'm caught unavoidably short. We duck into a darkened alleyway behind the Our Price record store and I have a wee against the wall. Finished, I turn to face the entrance of the alley, but the way is blocked by a couple of lads who are a few years older than us. I've never seen them before. One of them squares up to Alan and says, 'Were you looking at my friend like you fancy him?' Such are the excuses that thick thugs use to start fights.

He begins swinging at Alan and his mate sets about me. I take a jarring fist just below my left eye and that's enough for me. I've never been in a fight in my life and it doesn't occur to me to hit back. I just go down and stay down. I can't see Alan, but I suspect he does something similar. And we lie still on the ground until our assailants get bored and walk off, doubtless disappointed that they didn't have the chance to land a few more blows. We stay down for far longer than is strictly necessary, until we are absolutely certain that they have gone. We are both terrified.

We get up and, with barely a word exchanged, start running. And we don't stop until we clatter through the front door of the nearest police station – Gerald Road – about half a mile away. Where else would you go when you've been attacked? The officer on the front desk takes us seriously and treats us kindly. We are put into the back of a patrol car and driven around the local streets in search of the suspects. But there's no trace.

At home the following day, I stare into the mirror at the purpling bruise around my eye. For some strange reason, I feel rather proud of it.

*

In the autumn of 1988, I set out on three years of not working terribly hard at Reading University. I'm studying for a degree in human geography. Academia has never been my thing but I love the social life – the endless new friendships, the wide-open spaces between infrequent lectures, the chance to play football every week and the opportunity to discover that it only takes about four pints before the room starts to spin.

Dad comes to visit from time to time as he struggles to piece his life back together. He will be there for my graduation.

All the while, the policing idea continues to grow. When the Milk Round passes through the campus, it's the only presentation I go to. When the time comes, it will be the only job application I fill out.

*

I'm twenty years old, it's the summer of 1990, and I'm standing on the side of the Big Top stage at the Reading Festival. Despite an occasional and unfulfilled hankering to be a rock star – and a lifelong love of music – I'm not performing. But I am with the band. And it's one of the best feelings in the world as the crowd start bouncing.

The group in question rejoice in the name of Fat & Frantic and I've been with them on and off for three years or more. I started as a seventeen-year-old selling their T-shirts and now I'm doing the stage manager's job. Caught somewhere between Madness and The Housemartins in terms of style, they very nearly made it in the early nineties.

The members of the band are all five or six years older than me, but they've made me part of their family. And, with Dad gone and life in pieces, that is utterly priceless: a bunch of older men who let me join their adventure and who became both role models and friends. They still are. We all need people to look up to – people who share their lives with us and allow us to learn from their mistakes. People who love us for who we are. I don't quite know what I'd have done without them.

*

I'm still twenty. I'm in the West Country, spending the weekend with my new girlfriend and her family. Her mum is standing in the kitchen, asking me about my plans for the future. Assessing my suitability for her daughter. I tell her that I want to join the police. She just looks at me and says, 'You can do better with your life than that...'

*

It's 1991 and I'm twenty-one years old. I've graduated from university and my application for the Met has gone through. I've passed the initial interview and the subsequent assessment centre and now it's time for my Hendon fitness test.

Unfortunately, I have no upper-body strength to speak of. I can run all day, but the precise bio-mechanics required to perform a press-up remain a mystery to me. I've spent weeks attempting to master the art, but I still doubt myself. I'm standing tentatively in the gym with everyone else, sporting my red numbered bib. The Bleep Test is easy and I manage a perfectly respectable number of sit-ups. Now for the bit I'm dreading.

The PTIs stalk up and down as we assume the position. I reckon I need about thirty press-ups to be safe. The first ten are fine. The second ten are OK. But as I get into the early twenties, I begin to struggle. My arms are burning and beginning to shake, swiftly joined by the rest of my body. As I wobble my way up and down in painfully slow repetition, the voice of the Chief Instructor bellows out, military style, and directed straight at me: 'Number six, you're making me seasick...'

He savours those last two syllables, extending them for dramatic effect. My heart sinks.

Somehow though, I make it. I'm in.

*

Sunday, 20 September 1992. Weighed down with luggage, I get on the Northern Line at Kennington. It's the last time I will buy a Tube ticket. I'm on my way to Hendon, the most famous police-training college in the world. I'm nervous, excited, daunted, proud, overwhelmed, expectant, self-conscious. Imagining myself as a boy in blue.

III. *Johnny the Boy*

I'm met on the pavement outside Colindale Tube station by the magnificently moustachioed Sergeant Parkes. He's not hard to spot. He's the one in uniform.

Pleasantries exchanged, he piles a few of us into an unmarked white Transit van and drives us the short distance to Hendon, our new home for the next few months. We share a sense of apprehensive excitement as we wheel through the gates.

Yesterday, I was an ordinary member of the public. Tomorrow I will be a sworn police officer. Today, I find myself in the world between two worlds.

Initial formalities concluded, I find my room, way up high in one of the drab, grey slab tower blocks. Having made small talk with my immediate neighbours, I settle in and wonder how many of the previous residents have peed in my new sink.

The next morning, we assemble to take the oath.

*I, John Sutherland, do solemnly and sincerely declare and
affirm that I will well and truly serve our Sovereign Lady
the Queen in the office of Constable, without favour or
affection, malice or ill will; and that I will, to the best of my
power, cause the peace to be kept and preserved and prevent
all offences against the persons and properties of Her
Majesty's subjects and that while I continue to hold the said
office I will, to the best of my skill and knowledge, discharge
all the duties thereof faithfully according to the law.*

It will be the second most important set of promises I make
in my whole life.

*

There are sixty-odd of us in the six classes that make up the
'green' intake. The first couple of weeks are a bit of a blur.
Uniform fitting, self-defence training, first impressions
observed and offered, something well-intentioned but rather
dry about ethics and values and an introduction to drill with
a barking instructor. Fortunately, there are a couple of lads in
my class who are ex-Forces and they ease us into the whole
left-right-left thing.

I take possession of what is called PPE – my personal
protective equipment. The kit list isn't a long one, just a short
wooden stick and a pair of old-style chain-link handcuffs.
Oh, and a whistle. And that's it. No body armour – that's
a few years away still. No CS incapacitant spray – I'll need
to wait even longer for that. And no one has ever heard of
anything resembling a taser.

I'm allocated my first shoulder number, PC 565AB, and

I spend hours pinning individual letters and numbers onto assorted bits of uniform, in between the ironing and tunic defluffing that are essential before each morning's show parade.

Evening adjournments to the Peel Bar give us the opportunity to sink a few and tell the tales of our lives so far. My fellow probationers are a good bunch: an assortment of folk from all sorts of walks of life and old John who, at forty-seven, is the undisputed father of the house. We're all in this together.

*

Just a fortnight in and with next to no knowledge of anything that might be of operational use, we're turned out to our prospective divisions for an initial two-week taste of real policing and an introduction to some real police officers. Despite the warrant card carried proudly in my pocket, I won't feel like one of those for a good while yet.

My destination is Gerald Road nick, the very same station Alan and I had run to on the night we were attacked four years before. Tucked away in a little back street in the heart of Westminster, it's all hanging floral baskets and quiet reserve. It quickly becomes apparent to me that, generally speaking, nothing much happens there.

My brand-new winter trousers are itchy — proper finger-nails-down-the-blackboard uncomfortable. Turns out that a police uniform in the early 1990s isn't designed with comfort in mind. So I head out for my first shift in the real world, walking with one of the regular PCs, wearing a pair of rumpled pyjama bottoms underneath the pressed blue.

And I catch the uniformed reflection of myself in assorted windows.

*

In the second week, there's a break from the initial dry routine. I'm offered a back seat in Alpha 2, the local area car. We're allowed to take calls from further afield and I'm about to get stuck in. It's a 'late turn' – the shift starting at 2 p.m. and running until 10 p.m. – and we're already out and about when the mainset radio fitted to the car fires up: 'Units to deal please . . . Bush House, Aldwych, male armed with knives has taken a hostage inside the premises. More details to follow.'

The Scotland Yard operator assigns us to the call and the driver puts his foot down. Alpha 2 are running.

And this is what adrenalin feels like. The whoosh and surge of excitement and anticipation, newly experienced and thrilling biology, punched acceleration and jamming brakes. We're on the wrong side of the road and we're coming through at gathering speed, blues blazing and twos wailing. I'm being thrown around in the back. Damn, this is good.

We're not far off and we pull up at the same time as an Armed Response Vehicle. We're the first two units on scene and none of us can tell what's happening inside. Unknown threats.

My driver opens the boot of our car and hands me a large round perspex shield. I've never seen one before, but it doesn't occur to me to ask any questions. I just grab hold of it, sliding the large metal ring on the back over my left forearm, and follow his lead through the door of the famous old BBC building.

Once inside, we're told that a former employee with a grievance has got into an upstairs office and barricaded himself inside with a female member of staff. He's armed. And for the very first time, I'm headed straight into the heart of the story. I don't feel afraid.

Actually, it doesn't even occur to me to feel scared. I don't know enough and haven't experienced enough to know that 'afraid' might be a perfectly reasonable response in the circumstances. I'm just wide-eyed and utterly unaware of the implications of what's happening and of all the ways in which it might end. I don't think about the suspect. I don't think about his undoubtedly terrified victim. I don't think about the weapons. I just head up the stairs and into the adventure.

Our suspect and his prisoner are in a small inner office in the corner of a much larger room. They are just a matter of metres away from us, but silent and hidden from view behind opaque partition walls. There's no immediate way of telling what's happening inside.

Within a very short space of time, there are police officers everywhere. They include an important-looking commander who arrives on scene to take charge. None of them knows that I've only just started at Training School, and that I don't actually have the slightest idea what I'm doing. Neither of my Gerald Road colleagues seems concerned enough to mention it.

Whispered plans are drawn up to cover every eventuality, including the possibility of an emergency armed entry. For the latter to work, the advice is that the main room will need to be plunged into sudden darkness. And that, apparently, is where I come in.

My small part in the unfolding incident is to lie in the footwell of a huge old wooden desk – out of sight of the inner office, but within reach of the main light switch. I'm told to be ready for a command that might come at any moment, to leap out of my hiding place and hit the switch. And that's it, the sum total of my task.

I have no idea how long I'm under there but it's long enough to get really uncomfortable. I don't mind one bit though; I have a role, a non-speaking part, in the latest BBC drama. Eventually, someone takes pity on me and another officer gets a turn on the floor.

All ends well later that night and someone tells the commander that the young lad he sent to hide under the desk was a four-week novice from Hendon. He promptly writes me a letter, praising the 'calmness and professionalism' I had shown that night. And he tells me how the incident had been resolved:

You would probably like to know that the young lady was released suddenly at 22.15. The TSG [Territorial Support Group] seized their chance, overwhelmed the suspect and took from him three knives, including a Gurkha Kukri (a large knife with a broad blade about 12 inches long).

He sends a copy of his letter to Chief Superintendent Shew, the man in charge at the Training School. I am summonsed to Mr Shew's office and I feel the warmth of unexpected (and, let's be honest, not entirely unwelcome) attention. Are they really paying me to do this?

*

Back at Hendon, we settle into a rhythm of lessons and sport and drill, with an evening pint or two thrown in among exam-cramming and boot-bulling.

Early one morning, out on the stretch of private road that runs in front of the teaching block, we are finessing our marching technique. It would be fair to say that this doesn't form part of my natural skill set – a fact that does not go unnoticed. As we pass in front of the statue of Sir Robert Peel – the founder of the modern police service – the barking instructor singles me out for some loud, blunt feedback. Apparently, I'm going to need some more practice.

*

I open my first payslip. It's only a few hundred pounds, but it's significantly more money than I've ever earned in my life. I feel like a grown-up.

*

I still hate studying but, for the first time, it feels as though there's a purpose to it all. I'm learning stuff that's actually going to be useful. And I'm desperate to do well – to prove my worth, not least to myself.

On the ground-floor foyer of the main building, there's a display case containing a set of epaulettes for each rank in the Met, from constable to commissioner. Each time I pass, my eyes are drawn to the combination of insignia – star, crown and cross-tip staves – that are worn on the shoulders of the man at the top. I decide that's the job I want to do one day.

The twenty weeks of the course fly past as I soak up every new experience and, before I know where I am, we're marching round the main square in occasionally ragged formation on the day of our passing-out parade. Mum and a group of friends watch on. Dad isn't there.

Seated in the main hall afterwards, we listen to the speeches of the great and the good and watch as members of each class are called up to the stage to receive a selection of academic and merit awards. Then we come to something called the 'Baton of Honour'. The blurb in the programme says that it's given to the outstanding recruit in any intake, and the Chief Instructor gives it a bit of a build-up. Everyone's got their money on someone.

As the citation is read, parts of it begin to sound familiar. I look around me and catch one or two pairs of eyes. Eventually, the senior man looks up from his speaking notes and announces, in fine Scottish brogue: 'The Baton of Honour is awarded to PC Johnny Sutherland.'

My friend Jim, sitting up in the balcony, lets out a spontaneous and very loud cheer. I flush a shade of red and make my way forwards. It is the proudest moment of my young life.

After a week's contented leave, I arrive at Rochester Row Police Station for the start of my Street Duties Course – ten weeks of on-the-job continuation training, overseen by a sergeant and a group of more experienced PCs. It's time to learn the ropes for real.

At the end of our first briefing, I follow my tutor constable out of the front door and we turn left towards the busyness of Vauxhall Bridge Road. Once there, he turns to me and says, 'Right, I want you to stop a car.'

It's the simplest of tasks and it's his way of encouraging me into the shallow end of operational policing. I have the power to stop any vehicle on the road and I don't need any specific grounds in order to do so. I know and understand this, but I am suddenly terrified. Bizarrely, I hadn't given the BBC siege a second thought, but this has completely thrown me and I am now staring blankly at the one person I'm trying most to impress. I'm an unassuming man-boy and I'm suddenly overwhelmed by the thought of interrupting the busy day of an innocent motorist. What on earth am I going to say? What justification am I going to offer for the unsolicited intrusion?

I fumble and bumble my way through the very first use of my powers. Fortunately, the good-natured female driver doesn't seem to mind a bit. I'll get the hang of it eventually but, for now, I feel like a bit of an idiot. And, beneath my bright-eyed exterior, it's going to take some time to build my confidence. Batons of Honour don't count for much out here.

*

It is the start of a whole series of firsts, including my first nickname. They say that the only thing worse than having the mickey taken out of you is *not* having the mickey taken out of you. I'm a bit middle class and I talk a bit posh, so they call me Tarquin, Tarkers for short.

*

After my first vehicle stop comes my first traffic ticket. My first crime report, hand-written on large, colour-coded sheets, is followed by my first accident, my first pub fight, my first piece of lost property and my first set of directions given to another American tourist mangling the name of some great London landmark. Each is a small rite of passage – toddler steps in a policing life.

*

Everyone remembers their first arrest.

There are the good ones – the burglars, the drug dealers, the robbers and the men of violence. Then there's my one.

All I can manage is a drunk. No foot chase, no award-winning bravery, no outstanding display of investigative ability or policing streetcraft, just the discovery of a sad soul unable to take care of himself, lying on the piazza in front of Westminster Cathedral. He isn't even disorderly.

I help him up, put him into the back of the old Sherpa van and let him sleep it off in the cells. At least he's safe there.

Alcohol will be a recurring theme in so much of my policing life. Down the years, I will meet the fighting drunks, the happy drunks, the sleeping drunks and the falling down drunks. I will roll around on the ground with them and have my uniform torn by them. I will be hugged and serenaded by them. I will struggle to rouse them. I will peel them off the floor and help them back onto their hopelessly unsteady feet. Alcohol turns people into suspects, into flailing aggressors. It turns them into victims, into hapless and helpless incapables. And it turns them into addicts, into nine o'clock in the morning desperate drinkers. It turns them into pant-pissing shadows of themselves. If it was invented now, it would be illegal.

*

My first 'Sudden Death'. It's an early turn and we're called to a basement flat in a big old Pimlico townhouse. There are no suspicious circumstances, just some standard procedures to follow. I've never seen a dead body before.

Woody Allen once said that he wasn't afraid of death, just that he didn't want to be there when it happened. But, when it comes to the deaths of others, that's not a choice afforded to police officers.

My tutor leads me down the external staircase and we go in through the front door. The old man died in his living-room chair. We find his body sitting there, the tired old frame of a life, missing the artwork it once held. Everything else in the flat is just so – nothing out of place. We look for details of any relatives and an address or phone number for his doctor. We gather the medication lying on the sideboard and we bag up and seal a small assortment of cash and valuables.

My partner then decides he has better things to do and leaves me to get on with the rest of it. To be fair, there's nothing new or diverting for him here. Give it a bit of time and you lose count of the dead you've seen. So now there is only silence: just me and a body, waiting for the undertaker to arrive. It's ever so slightly unsettling for a young lad who hasn't seen much of the world. The skittish part of me is half expecting the old boy to cough at any moment, or to scare me witless in some other way. More than anything, though, the thought I can't shake is that he died on his own. There was no one there to hold his hand, to say that they cared, to ask if he needed anything to make himself more comfortable. I only hope that it wasn't long and drawn out, that he didn't feel too much pain. No one should have to die alone.

*

That's the one consolation when I turn up to the next one. It's another early turn and I'm in a small flat just off Vincent Square. A wife woke up this morning and her husband didn't. There he is, still lying in their bed, not a breath in his ample body. And I am the passing stranger in uniform, attempting to offer some sort of comfort on the worst day of her life. Each little story stays with me. Each leaves a mark on my soul.

*

Some calls have an altogether happier ending.

It's an autumn morning and we're racing to a ground-floor apartment in one of the Georgian terraces just round the corner from Pimlico Tube station. An elderly lady has fallen at home and is unable to get up. Fortunately, she had kept her personal alarm within reach and was able to send a distress call. In job parlance, this sort of situation is known as a 'collapse behind locked doors' and, as police officers, we have the legal power to force entry to any building in order to save life.

We arrive on scene and encounter an immediate problem. The lady has fallen just behind her front door, ruling that out as the entry point. Any impact on the door would inevitably cause further damage to her already frail body. I push the letter box open to offer some words of reassurance. She is conscious and able to reply. I tell her that, one way or another, we'll get to her. But we need another way in and time is of the essence.

It rapidly becomes clear that the only alternative is a ground-floor window that faces out onto the street. But, between pavement and glass, there is a chest-high iron railing and an open basement that's four or five feet wide.

One of my ever-resourceful colleagues borrows a ladder from a neighbour and we lay it across the gap, resting one end on the window sill and anchoring the other on the top of the railings. It's safe enough.

I'm given a leg up and start to crawl across on all fours. And, for a brief moment, I might be back in my childhood, climbing across the rafters of a barn with Titus.

An ambulance has arrived and a paramedic readies himself to follow me across. But first the window. This is the fun bit. I reach into my right-hand trouser pocket and pull out my wooden truncheon. This will be the first meaningful action it has seen. Taking care not to get glass in my eyes, I break in – a couple of good blows with my stick are all that's required. I pull the jagged edges of the glass out of the side of the frame and someone passes me a blanket to lay across the bottom of it.

I crawl through with the paramedic behind me and find myself in the lady's bedroom. I call out to explain to her what's happening as I begin to crunch across the glass-strewn carpet.

I open the bedroom door and there she is, utterly helpless

on the hallway floor. And we've got to her in time. She is in a good deal of pain, but there's relief in her eyes. The paramedic crouches down next her and begins the process of putting her back together.

As the ambulance departs for the hospital, I have a chance to survey the damage we've done. Smashing windows with good cause is one of those guilty pleasures that this line of work affords from time to time.

But saving a life? Well, that's the greatest thing of all.

*

Constant shift working can't be good for you. It's like living with semi-permanent jet lag. A future girlfriend will complain that I seem to be tired all the time. Early turn is my least favourite. Waking up is never easy to do – at least, not at five in the morning. That said, I look forward to lates and to nights in particular. Generally speaking, the more exciting and challenging things tend to happen in the latter part of the day and after dark. And, at the end of a long night, as you crawl under the duvet, there is a sense of quiet satisfaction in knowing that the rest of the working world is just setting out on the morning commute.

*

During the first part of this particular night shift, nothing much has been happening and I've been watching the slow turn of the hands. But I hear reports coming through on the radio of an accident somewhere up near Hyde Park Corner. Then I hear my sergeant calling for me to head up there to help out. As the probationer, when I'm not making tea for the team, I'm expected to complete the routine paperwork at the scene of any incident or crime.

But 'accident' would be entirely the wrong word to describe what has happened.

As I turn the corner into Knightsbridge, I see a Fiat Panda rolled onto its side by the westbound kerb, about a hundred yards down from the junction with Grosvenor Place. And there's the motionless body of a man lying in the middle of the road. A handful of yards to the right, a Ford Sierra is wrapped round the central reservation, also on the westbound side, but facing into the oncoming traffic. There are two people trapped inside it.

The man lying in the road was the driver of the Panda, an Italian living and working in London. He was simply going about his business, making his way home at the end of the day. And now he's dead. The randomness of it all.

Someone covers his body with a bright-red blanket sourced from the back of an ambulance.

The Sierra was stolen in Reading and was being driven at lunatic speeds on the wrong side of the road. It was head on and the Italian didn't have a chance. Behind the wheel of the stolen car is a drunken teenager. His right leg has snapped clean in half, the ragged end of his thigh bone poking through the surface of his skin. His passenger is a homeless alcoholic along for the ride and now emptying his bowels on the front seat. The fire brigade will cut them both out, and they will both survive.

Passing pedestrians and traffic slow to observe the scene, but quickly move on with life, as we remain and contend with death. After the initial flurry of activity – putting cordons in, redirecting traffic, marshalling the other emergency services and hunting for any witnesses – things have just started to settle down when I notice a man with a camera standing over the covered body of the Italian, taking photographs. I'm disbelieving. Has he no conscience or shame?

I go over to him and tell him to leave. He says that he's a press photographer and mentions the national tabloid paper he's from. He tells me that his readers have a right to see what's happened here tonight. I politely, but firmly, show him to the blue-and-white tape further down the road and tell him to move on. He's ignored a police cordon. He's interfering with a major crime scene. And he seems to have no concept of the dignity of the dead.

No more than ten minutes later, I look over and see that the photographer is back, exactly where he was before, taking more pictures. He has made the considerable walk all the way around the block and found his way back inside the secure area at the other end of the road. I'm a fairly mild-mannered sort of person, always have been, and I've properly lost my temper just a handful of times in my whole life. This is one of them. I grab hold of him and begin forcibly shoving him down the road. He starts hissing threats, saying that he's going to sue me. I actually don't care. He's crossed a line, in every sense of the phrase. All in the pursuit of bad news, of a grisly picture, of a payout, of some kind of twisted titillation. Is that really how the world works?

Photojournalist dispatched, I'm told to go with the boy driver to hospital. Later that night, I accompany him into the operating theatre (part evidential requirement, part fascination with the unknown) and I'm given a heavy lead apron to wear, protection afforded to the vitals from the worst effects of X-rays. I watch as the foot of the broken limb is lifted into a hoist and then, amazed, as the surgeon sets about it with what looks like a camping mallet. No dignity or ceremony, just a lot of hammering. And I feel no pity for him. There's a large part of me reckoning he deserves this.

My thoughts wander. Maybe, just maybe, there isn't enough of the anaesthetic in his system and maybe, just maybe, he's feeling some real pain at the end of his homicidal night's work. Not terribly compassionate of me.

*

It's not all dead bodies.

It's the first half of another night duty, just a couple of hours into the shift. I'm the operator in a marked Metro and we're driving through the back streets close to Victoria Station. A car edges out of a side street up in front of us and we decide to give it a pull. No immediate reason beyond the late hour and location, but the radio is quiet and you have to cast a line to catch a fish.

I get out and invite the driver to join me on the pavement. He's a well-appointed and extremely well-spoken individual in his late fifties or early sixties. I ask him whether he's had anything to drink, the usual routine, and he mentions that he had a glass of wine earlier on. So I ask him politely to take a breath test. A suspicion that he might have alcohol in his system is all I need to make the request. Actually, it's more of a requirement than a request.

His demeanour changes immediately and he flatly refuses. And we find ourselves at an impasse. I'm not going to change my mind and he's not going to change his. But I have the advantage of knowing that the law is on my side. He tells me that he is a member of the House of Lords. I tell him that I am arresting him for failing to provide a breath test.

We go through the same routine at the station. The sergeant tells him to blow into the machine. He declines. Inevitably, he gets charged and sent to court. It turns out that membership of the upper house is not an established defence in law.

*

On 20 October 1993, just over a year into my policing career, PC Patrick Dunne is murdered. He was a local community officer based in south London who was shot dead when investigating the sounds of gunfire just off Clapham High Street. I had never met him but, somehow, I knew him. He was a uniformed copper just like me and that made him family. His death hit me unexpectedly hard.

The impact is reinforced the following month, when I take possession of the keys to my first home. I've been saving every available penny for the past year and have enough for a small deposit, some furniture and the assorted pots and pans needed by every first-time buyer. I move out of the cupboard-sized spare room at Mum's place and find myself the proud owner of a two-bed, first-floor flat on the edge of Brixton. It's no more than a quarter of a mile from the place where Pat was gunned down. Each time I walk past the scene, I pay my silent respects.

On 9 February 1994, Sergeant Derek Robertson is murdered. He was stabbed when attempting to arrest a robbery suspect and died of his injuries. He will later be awarded a posthumous Queen's Gallantry Medal for his extraordinarily courageous actions. I never had the honour of knowing Derek but, like Pat, he was part of who and what I now am. And I mourn him.

The following morning, as I stare at his picture on the front of the paper, my tears smudge the newsprint. Sometimes, police officers pay the greatest price of all.

*

I settle into the rhythm and routine of life at Belgravia. I'm not a natural street cop. I don't have the inherent abilities of the PCs who consistently make outstanding crime arrests. They seem to have a set of instincts that can't be taught. But I do work hard. I volunteer for every call, offer to take the dull shifts as jailer and station officer and generally do whatever I can to prove my worth. I realise over time that this is one of the quieter postings in London, that there are any number of other places that would be more exciting to work in. I look for new opportunities and experiences wherever possible.

*

My favourite TV programme has to be *BBC Sports Personality of the Year* and this year, it's being filmed at the QEII Conference Centre in Westminster. I happen to be on lates. I keep out of trouble during the first part of the shift and, as evening draws in, I find my way to the top of Victoria Street and to the front of the venue. If anyone asks, I'm here to deal with potential crowd-control issues. If anyone actually wants to know, I'm here to see my heroes.

Later that evening, I'm in the station office at Belgravia when a famous figure stumbles through the front door. He's a BBC presenter who has clearly taken full advantage of the free bar at the after-show party. He's here to plead for the release of a colleague who couldn't hold his booze quite as well and who has, consequently, been arrested for being drunk and disorderly. He is now sobering up in the cells. The presenter stands at the front counter and makes the case for the defence. In his mind, he might well sound coherent – out loud, marginally less so. And he sways as he speaks. He's admirably persistent and ever so slightly repetitive, but I am unmoved. Reluctantly, he concedes defeat and shuffles back out into the night. Watching certain programmes will never be quite the same again.

*

Christmas. Just as the nation's children are climbing into bed on Christmas Eve – all shining eyes and anticipation – I'm getting changed for work. And, just as the nation's families are waking up on Christmas morning – all tearing paper and squeals of excitement – I'm pulling my duvet up over my head. The gift I receive from my colleagues is a new nickname. JTB. Johnny the Boy.

*

One morning, three of us are sent on an errand to Brixton Police Station. Three young PCs sent to collect some property. Two of us are white, one of us is black. All of us are in plain clothes. We walk into the back yard at LD (every station in London has a two-letter code and LD is the one for Brixton). There's a uniformed PC slouched lazily against the railings outside the back door of the station. One or two of his colleagues are milling around. The lazy one looks over towards us and, with his eye on my black colleague, says casually, 'Spot the prisoner...'

That's it. He's not aggressive, just snide and weasully. None of us responds and it takes several seconds for me to understand what's just been said. I lack the confidence to speak up. To anyone. I regret it. I should have checked that my friend was OK. And I should have called out the bigot in blue.

*

It's another early start, and a group of us are due to head out on patrol in a carrier. One of the PCs was out last night and he turns up for parade still drunk. I'm not sure he's even been to bed. He's stumbling and he's slurring, but rather than send him home, the skipper bundles him into the back of the van as we all head out expecting another dull morning.

We pick up a call to a vulnerable man on Westminster Bridge, possibly threatening to jump, and the early morning mist makes for an eerie scene as we pull up in the shadow of Big Ben. The inebriated PC gets out and wants to do the talking. Someone sees sense and he's tipped straight back into the carrier. And it's just not funny. We're not always as professional as we claim to be.

That's a sentiment that applies just as much to me as it does to any of my colleagues.

On another morning, I'm out in uniform with the rest of my team and we're taking part in a road check on Millbank, a busy main road next to the River Thames. We're using our powers under the Road Traffic Act to stop a succession of vehicles in the hunt for possible offences. I'm still finding my feet as a young copper and I still want to impress my colleagues. I stop a car, glance at the out-of-date tax disc displayed in the lower corner of the windscreen and begin to give the driver a proper dressing down. I am pompous and condescending – lapsing into that unpleasant stereotype of an overbearing police officer lacking the maturity or the professionalism to use their powers wisely or well. My behaviour finds me out immediately.

The driver looks at me with an expression of anxious bewilderment. 'But officer,' he says quietly, 'it's not out of date.'

My heart drops and I check the front of the car to see that he's absolutely right. I have made a complete fool of myself. I apologise unreservedly. There's nothing else I can do and I feel both horrified and ashamed – not that I've been caught out, but that I could have behaved that way in the first place.

The thing is, it's just not who I am. The vast majority of police officers I will work with as the years go by are not like that either. In my mind, later the same day, I listen back to the exchange with the poor driver and promise myself that I will never speak to anyone in that way again. There are times as a police officer when you need to be forceful – when there is no time to be mucking around or mincing words. But there is never any excuse for being an idiot.

*

The IRA are still active on the mainland at this early point in my policing career. Hyde Park and Harrods are recent enough history and, in 1991, I had watched the news reports following the mortar strike on Downing Street. The attacks, large and small, keep coming.

In November 1992, two months after I started at Hendon, officers in north London pulled over a van containing a massive IED. One of the PCs was shot as he challenged the two terrorist occupants. He survived. They escaped.

In April 1993, at the time I was doing my Street Duties Course, the murderous Bishopsgate bombers devastated a whole swathe of the City.

Perhaps unsurprisingly then, much of my formative time as a PC is given to security patrols in central London. As many as two shifts in every three are spent on dedicated beats as the first line of defence against prospective attack. I have my wooden stick, a pair of handcuffs and an old Storno radio. They have a seemingly endless arsenal of weaponry and explosives. Truth is, though, it doesn't feel noble or dangerous. It is just mind-numbingly, soul-destroyingly dull: short fixed patrols in streets where nothing ever happens, hoping that a colleague in a vehicle will take pity on you in the middle of the night and run you up to the Bagel Shop in Brick Lane. I understand why we have to do it and there's no way of knowing what we prevent while we're out there, but it isn't what I joined to do. The fact is, I'm bored. Somewhere in the back of my unfulfilled mind, I even wonder whether this policing life is for me.

But, looking back, I never came close to walking away. The fact is that policing had already got under my skin, to a far greater extent than perhaps I realised as I meandered up and down a deserted Birdcage Walk at three o'clock in the morning.

The previous summer, I'd heard a friend tell a story about Sir Christopher Wren, the architect responsible for the design of St Paul's. It went something like this: Sir Christopher, dressed in casual clothing and without identifying himself, paid a visit to the site where the great building was still under construction. He saw three stonemasons at work and approached each in turn to ask them what they were doing. The first two provided straightforward, factual answers: 'I'm shaping this piece of stone.'

'I'm helping to construct this section of the wall.'

Then he approached the third man and put the same question to him: 'Can I ask you what you're doing?' said the architect.

'Sir, I'm building a cathedral,' came the reply.

As soon as I heard it, I loved it. I still do.

I have always wanted to be part of something big, something important, something significant, something that matters. And policing is all of those things.

*

Night duty and a blessed break from the counter-terrorism patrols. I must be in the sergeant's good books, because he's posted me as operator on one of the cars. One of the senior PCs is driving – a man with a large beard and a large stomach.

We head out and I'm full of expectation. Maybe I'll get a decent crime arrest in tonight. My more experienced colleague can show me how it's done. He pilots us to the little road behind the Victoria Palace Theatre and stops at the junction with Bressenden Place. He switches the engine off. Excellent, I think to myself, we're watching for stolen cars or suspicious no-gooders, poised eagerly to respond. But that isn't his line of thinking. Without a word to me, he settles back in his seat, closes his eyes. And falls asleep.

I just sit there, lacking the confidence to challenge him, not daring to imitate him.

There are some consistent themes emerging. I'm not entirely sure of myself, of who I am. I want to be accepted and I don't want to rock the boat. Or wake the driver.

*

Some of the team manage to stay awake on duty, only to fall asleep on the way home. Simon is my favourite case in point. He lives a few stops down the main line from Victoria Station, just a short hop at the end of the working day. He and a few of the lads go out for a drink or three at the end of a late turn and he catches the last train out of town. Perfect timing, except that he falls asleep and misses his stop, misses several stops in fact. When he finally stirs, he's at the end of the line in Brighton and there are no more trains running for the night. He spends a few draughty and uncomfortable hours on the platform until, finally, the early Milk Train sets off in the direction of the capital.

The problem is that by now a pattern has been established. Simon promptly falls asleep again and doesn't wake up until he's back in Victoria, at the exact spot where his ill-starred journey began the night before. It keeps the rest of us laughing for days.

*

Over the course of my career, I will police any number of football matches. But only ever one Test match. It's the summer of 1994 and England are playing South Africa at Lord's, the home of cricket. The home team are in the field and their bowlers are being hit to all corners of the ground. My posting is on the boundary rope, more or less at the point that those in the know refer to as 'deep fine leg'. It's not a bad place to spend the working day. I'm told to sit down on a funny little chair with no legs and to take my hat off, ensuring that I don't obstruct the view of the paying customers. My job seems to be to watch the field of play. In case of streakers, I suppose. And that's about it.

So I settle down to enjoy the game or, rather, the summary lesson in sporting excellence being handed out by the visiting team. I think England manage to take two wickets in the entire day. The consolation is that I get a close-up view of one of them. Angus Fraser is fielding about ten yards away from me. His South African opponent miscues his shot and the ball's high in the air for a seeming eternity. Fraser steadies himself as the crowd hold their breath. I'm with them. As he hangs on to the catch, I completely forget myself. In full uniform, minus the hat of course, I raise both arms in celebration and join the joy of the crowd.

It's then that I realise that I must be on TV, with replays available around the world. I sit on my hands and hope that my sergeant wasn't watching.

*

I don't know how many straight men have been the victims of homophobia, but I would have to number myself among

47

them. What is, on my part, a completely innocent invite to a male colleague to stay over after a night out, is misinterpreted as a sexual advance. I think I'm being hospitable. He thinks I'm trying to get him into bed. I don't have a girlfriend at the moment and the presumption among my colleagues seems to be that I must be looking for a boyfriend. This is the early 1990s and the Met Police isn't the only bit of society struggling to keep up with the sexual revolution. Not many coppers have come out and, having lived an uncommonly blinkered life up to this point, I don't have any close gay friends. At least, none that I know of.

One of the other PCs on my team has the decency to speak to me. We're walking along Buckingham Palace Road, back towards the station. 'John, can I ask you a personal question?'

'Of course.'

'Do you prefer girls or boys?'

I don't mind him asking and I don't mind answering. But I realise that everyone else has been talking. About me, not to me. It's unsettling. And it all comes as I'm getting ready to move to a new borough. I've been feeling for a while that I need a change of scene and I've been looking for something more challenging. Posters advertising my leaving drinks have begun to appear around the place.

A few days after the boy/girl conversation, I'm walking down the main stairs and I look up at the big notice board on the first-floor landing. There's one of my posters, the same as all the others, except for a single word scrawled in black pen on the bottom of it: 'Faggot'. And no one had challenged it or thought to take the poster down. Silence is collusion, as one of my old bosses used to say.

I have no idea how to respond and I will never find out who is responsible. But should I allow the ignorance of a handful of colleagues to define my experience of – or belief in – an organisation? Setting aside personal discomfort, the answer surely has to be no.

Policing – who we are and what we do – matters far too much to allow it to be undermined or damaged by an unconscionable minority. This great, shared endeavour is so much more significant than the opinions or behaviour of any one of them.

Sir, I'm building a cathedral.

IV. *Closer to Home*

After two years wandering the streets of Belgravia, I take up a new role in Lambeth, south of the river. If my first posting had brought me, on occasions, to the point of questioning whether policing was for me, the move closer to home removes every last trace of doubt, with emphatic immediacy. I see and experience more in my first two weeks in Brixton than I have in the entirety of the last two years in Westminster, beginning with my first set of lates and my first murder. A domestic.

I still remember her name.

*

It's early evening, halfway through the shift. My more experienced colleague and I are sitting in the canteen at Brixton. There's a plate of half-eaten food on the table in front of me when the call comes out. A member of the public has dialled 999 to say that they've discovered the dead body of a relative in a flat just off Coldharbour Lane. She appears to have been stabbed.

We throw our chairs back, abandon our meals and sprint down the corridor to the stairs and the ground floor. The address that's been given is not too far away and we're determined to be there first. Into the back yard and we pile into the car. I hold my radio with one hand and the front passenger door with the other as my teammate speeds us round the back streets of Lambeth. My heart and head are racing in time with the car – driven by a sense of urgency, of purpose, of duty, of anticipation, of excitement even.

We pull up outside and I scramble through the gate. I have no real sense of what I'm going to find on the inside. This is completely new territory. I've seen any number of dead bodies by now, but I've never been to the scene of a murder. The address is one of those old Victorian terrace conversions and the call is to the maisonette occupying the top two floors. The staircase runs straight ahead from the open front door before doubling back on itself. In we go.

As I turn the corner halfway up, I see her body, face down and lifeless on the landing in front of me. There's no need to check for vital signs. Sometimes it's just obvious. She has been stabbed repeatedly in the throat. The carpet is old and dirty and dark in colour. It absorbs and conceals the extent of the blood.

There are times and places and moments that you can never un-remember.

I pause for just a few seconds before, batons drawn, my partner and I search the premises, room by room. We are looking for suspects or for some poor soul who might have been witness to the carnage. God forbid there were any children present.

We move carefully, tense and watchful. But the flat is empty and everything begins to slow a little, including my heartbeat. Everyone else has heard the call and is beginning to turn up now. Soon, there are uniforms everywhere. Colleagues go to work outside, locking the house down, putting cordons in place, speaking to the original informant and beginning to knock on neighbours' front doors. No one wants to contaminate the scene any more than is absolutely essential so, as the man already inside, I remain. The fewer the sets of boots that tread through, the better our chances of preserving and retrieving any evidence that might be here.

I stand silently beside the young woman's prone form, notebook open, drawing a simple sketch of what I can see. And she just lies there. I don't know what I think. I'm simply concentrating on doing what I'm told, on learning from those around me, on absorbing every last detail of the experience. Perhaps the fact that I can't see her face makes it all seem a little less real; makes it a little less personal. But, at the age of twenty-five, this is already more of life – and death – than I have ever seen before.

Specialists from the Murder Team begin to arrive: the Crime Scene Manager, a SOCO – Scenes of Crime Officer – and a photographer. The CSM is usually a detective sergeant and he or she oversees the detailed police investigation at the scene. The SOCO is responsible for forensics – fingerprints, blood samples, strands of hair, fragments of fibre and so much more besides. The photographer takes video and stills of everything. Between them, they begin to piece together the nightmare that happened here.

When my own work at the address is done, I leave them and head back to the station for the first briefing with the Senior Investigating Officer. I'm the youngest and least experienced in a room full of seasoned cops, but as the first on scene, I'm given the floor and asked to describe all we have done from the moment the call came out until now. They listen as I tell my story. I'm told that I'll be required at the post mortem the following morning. I'm to be the 'Continuity Officer' – the one with the duty of confirming that the body lying under unforgiving light is the same one I discovered at the scene.

Back in my own flat at the end of the shift, I turn it all over in my mind. Today has been more demanding, more desperate, more compelling, more fulfilling, somehow more thrilling than anything I have ever done before. And yet for the friends and family who are now in mourning it has been the most horrifying and shattering of days, beyond description or comprehension. For one young woman, it has been the end of everything. As a police officer, you have to be careful what you wish for.

I'm not sure how much sleep I get before I make my way to the mortuary the following morning. Too many thoughts jostling and too many images passing through my mind.

The DI from the murder team is there already. He's an old hand and meets me outside, offering me some Vicks VapoRub to put under my nose. That will be the smell I remember at the end of the day. The building itself is dull and nondescript – a place of science and evidence, as far removed from a chapel of rest as it's possible to be. The DI leads me into the room where she is lying on the slab.

I can see her face now – blank and bloodless.

I make my identification and stay for a while, part transfixed and part horrified by the desperate and essential indignities that follow.

They catch him in the end. He's a former boyfriend – a man of unimaginable violence, the inhabitant of a world beyond my comprehension.

*

I'm still in my first full week at Brixton. It's the middle of the afternoon as calls come in about a serious assault on Stockwell Road, just along from the old skate park. For now, I'm the only person available.

I make my way hurriedly on foot and see the victim lying on the pavement in front of the parade of shops just ahead on the right. As I approach, I can see the full extent of his injuries. He's conscious and still breathing, but his throat has been sliced wide open from his right ear all the way round to his larynx, a visceral mix of blood and sinew and tissue – like something from a too-graphic novel. And not for the faint hearted. I keep him still, call up for more help and hold on for the ambulance.

He's rushed off to A&E with one of my colleagues for company and the scene and investigation are handed over to the CID. I've no idea what happens to him – whether he makes a full recovery, whether those responsible are identified, whether justice is served. I don't even know who he is.

My part in his life has been confined to a few brief words and a few short minutes, played out on a south London street.

I walk back to the station to get the paperwork done – and the world keeps turning. That's how it will be for so much of the next twenty years: snapshots of sorrow and on to the next thing.

*

A couple of days later, there's another murder, just off Kings Avenue on the edge of Clapham. I don't even make it to this one – I'm already tucked up with another job.

*

I'm not sure how I feel about all the things I'm seeing and dealing with. Typical bloke. In the thick of it all, when I'm on scene and working, there's precious little time for emotion. In the periods of relative quiet that follow, I'm not sure how much space I allow for it. I tell the stories to captivated friends and first-time acquaintances and I am carried along by the adventure of it all. And the deep feelings just get buried away. The contents of a time capsule awaiting discovery at some indeterminate point in the future.

*

My second murder scene is another domestic. Late turn again. I'm the operator in the station van when the call comes out and we're a long way off. Other members of the team get there quite a bit before we do.

The desperation is unfolding in the block of flats on the left at the top of Brixton Hill, just by the main traffic lights. We arrive and make our way upstairs. The victim, a young blonde woman, was still conscious when the first officers arrived. She was even able to say a few words. But, by the time I get there, she's fading away. She's been stabbed several times and she's slumped on the floor at the foot of the bed, surrounded by colleagues doing what they can for her. There's blood everywhere and bandages scattered all around, as words of reassurance are being spoken to an ebbing soul.

'Stay with us now.'

'We're going to look after you.'

'The ambulance is on the way.'

'You're going to be OK.'

The suspect – her boyfriend – is still at the scene. I find him sitting, glassy eyed, on the living-room sofa, deeply disturbed and staring into the void. At one end of the corridor, she's losing her struggle for life. At the other end, he's losing his mind. Caught between the two of them are a bunch of police officers, doing the very best they can.

The paramedics join us. There's no space for a stretcher, so she is lifted onto a lightweight chair that's been brought up from the back of the ambulance. I grab the handles as one of the medics grabs the footrest. Her body lolls between us as we stumble-rush down stairwells to the ground floor. Time is everything now and there's no dignity, only desperation. Then the mad run to the hospital.

In through clattering doors and urgently raised voices to the Resus Room. Despite the trauma of the unfolding human tragedy, there's a need for clear heads. For our part, there's a pressing need to think about evidence. If she doesn't make it, our duty is to make sure that he doesn't get away with it. We need a pre-transfusion blood sample, one that we can compare accurately with the scene – one that hasn't been contaminated by hospital supplies. And we need to preserve her clothing and any other items of potential significance to the investigation that will follow. For these reasons, we remain close by.

I stand there and I see the open-heart surgery: the brave and brilliant and ultimately hopeless efforts of the A&E staff to save her life. Everyone gives everything. And everything isn't enough.

I put my arm round the shoulder of the colleague next to me – now broken down and weeping, undone by the horror of it all.

By the time I get home, it's far too late to talk to the friends who live a more conventional sort of life. My flatmate was in bed long before I got in. So I lean against the cupboards in the quietness of the kitchen and begin to work my way through a packet of cigarettes. These things stay with you for ever.

*

Two domestic murders in the space of a few weeks. And that's just one London borough, just when I was on duty. A staggering proportion of the killings we deal with every year are domestics. The same holds true for violent crime of every kind. Survivors of domestic violence are among the most vulnerable repeat victims in any community, likely to be assaulted and abused on dozens of occasions before we get called for the first time. And while we've made some progress in our understanding of the impact of domestic violence on its immediate victims, I don't think we've come anywhere close to properly comprehending – much less responding to – the secondary impact on the children growing up in homes where violence is a daily reality.

Domestic violence is terrorism on an epic scale, a disease of pandemic proportions and the single greatest cause of harm in society.

*

I live just off one end of Acre Lane. Brixton nick is close to the other. In most jobs, living a fifteen-minute walk from the office would be considered an advantage. In policing, that isn't always the case.

I head in on foot for a late turn and make my way down to the basement changing room. I take off my prized black leather jacket and hang it on the corner of my locker door. And I see a large mouthful of gob dripping like treacle down the back of it – a gift from a hostile stranger who knows what I do. But not who I am.

*

Some working days turn out to be less about disaster and more about adventure. I'm in the front passenger seat of an unmarked police car with a couple of plain-clothes colleagues. Gavin is driving and we find ourselves somewhere near the top of Brixton Hill. We're stopped at a T-junction when a moped crosses from left to right in front of us. Young rider, dressed casually and wearing a helmet. Gavin and I look at each other and say, almost simultaneously, 'That's nicked.' It's just instinct, but somehow we both know.

And we're off after him. Nice and easy does it – he doesn't know we've seen him. Southbound, towards Christchurch

Road. Onto the radio, I call up for a check on the number plate. It comes back stolen and we're in business.

Right onto Christchurch Road and towards the junction with Brixton Hill, he still hasn't seen us. Everyone else has heard the result of the check and they're all heading our way. Someone on the radio asks for India 99 – the helicopter. Having them overhead makes it easier to track a moving suspect and their thermal imaging equipment can pick up signs of life in the most unlikely of hiding places.

Straight over the junction, eastbound onto Streatham Place. Approaching the next set of lights.

Now he's seen us.

Left into New Park Road. And immediately left again into an estate – Hayes Court, I think. He drops the bike while the engine is still running. I've got my door open before we've stopped moving. He's off and I'm after him.

Damn, he's quick.

Through the estate and back out onto Streatham Place. I'm trying my best to keep up. At least this stretch is downhill. Then, up ahead, I see some members of the public walking towards us. I shout out: 'Police . . . Stop, police . . .'

Gavin has joined the chase – he's come through the other side of Hayes Court. It must be blindingly obvious to people what's happening, but no one does a thing to help. Not a thing. Perhaps they don't care. Perhaps they're afraid of the consequences of getting involved. Maybe they're just pleased to see someone getting away from the Old Bill.

Our suspect is out across the two nearside lanes of the road and over the central reservation. Now onto the far side of the road, he rounds a corner and vanishes into another estate. I follow him, but I've lost sight of him.

By this time, the helicopter is up and there are units running from all over the place. Everyone wants a part of the chase.

I keep going, but he's nowhere to be seen. I'm blowing heavily. So is Gavin. We walk forwards slowly. There are something like a dozen stairwells and cut-throughs to choose from. Neither of us looks or feels particularly hopeful. I choose the first set of stairs on my right, for no other reason than the fact that it's the closest. I have no real expectations, but, two flights up, there he is, crouched against the wall and breathing just as hard as me. I've got just about enough puff to tell him that he's nicked and to put the handcuffs on. I shout to Gavin and, for a precious moment, smile to myself. It's a decent crime arrest – and I've had a full audience on the radio.

Twenty minutes later, I walk proudly into custody with my prisoner. I'll never be the world's greatest thief taker, but I got my man today.

*

If you're paying attention, policing has something new to teach you every day.

Edmond Locard was a leading French forensic scientist in the first half of the twentieth century and he gave his name to a concept that remains fundamental to the detection of crime in the twenty-first century. Locard's Principle says, very simply, 'Every contact leaves a trace.' It means that, wherever there is contact between two objects, an exchange takes place.

Take a burglar, for example. When he breaks into a house, he leaves traces of himself behind at the scene: a footprint in a flowerbed, blood or clothing fibres on the jagged edge of the broken windowpane, fingerprints on the cupboard doors. And he takes traces of the scene away with him: mud on the soles of his shoes, microscopic fragments of glass all over his clothes, the jewellery he's stolen. Locard's Principle offers an insight into how so many of the most serious crimes – certainly those that aren't able to rely on eye-witness evidence – get solved. Evidence left by the suspect at the scene; evidence from the scene carried by the suspect. Because every contact leaves a trace.

And if you think about it a little more, Locard's Principle might equally be applied to every kind of human inter-action. Every time two people come into contact with one another – whether lifelong friends or passing strangers – an exchange takes place. For better or for worse. We smile or we scowl; we encourage or we ignore; we knock down or we help up; we show gratitude or we dismiss; we are angry or we forgive; we bless or we curse; we give or we take; we love or we hate. If the principle holds true, then the challenge, for police officers patrolling the streets and for all the rest of us, is to consider what kind of trace we want to leave behind.

Taking the idea further still, I will – much further down the line – reflect on the deep impact my working life is having on me. This job brings you into repeated contact with every form of human sadness: death and grief, wickedness and violence, the lonely, the lost and the hurting. These are not remote things encountered by other people in circumstances

beyond my understanding. They are not softened by conveni-
ent distance or filtered through the lens of the media. They
are right there in front of me – immediate and overwhelming
and heart-breaking and shattering.

And every contact leaves a trace.

*

Of all the people policing brings you into contact with, some
leave more of an impression than others. Invariably for all
the wrong reasons.

It's mid-1990s Brixton and, at times, it seems as though
one particular woman is in the cells every day. Her name is
Julie. You can tell from looking at her that she was once a
beautiful young woman. Genuinely so. And she's still only in
her early twenties. But she's hooked on crack – a desperate
addict, turning tricks in alleyways for desperate men.

She staggers through the custody suite in knee-length
boots that are falling apart, wearing filthy, dishevelled clothes.
She has red, dead eyes and dirt and snot are smeared across
her face. Then there's the smell. Oh the smell . . . The husk of
a life.

*

Another junkie in custody. A sad soul with a vacant stare
and terrible skin. I wonder what his story is? Everyone has a
story and it's too easy to write people off just because of the
state they're in.

My job today is to strip search him. Together with a colleague, I take the suspect to the privacy of an empty cell to
do the necessary.

I am conscious of the fact that you should always take

good care when you search a user, so I ask him very clearly, 'Have you got any needles on you?'

'No.'

'Are you sure?'

'Yes.'

My first mistake is to take him at his word. My second is that I don't bother to put gloves on. My third is that I put my hand straight into his trouser pocket without patting it down properly first. All my own stupid fault.

The needle goes straight into the palm of my hand. I feel a flush of cold go through me. I jerk my hand away and utter some sort of expletive. My colleague knows instantly what's happened and nothing is said, then or later, but I know that he is fully expecting me to punch the prisoner in the face. The thing is, I'm just not the punchy kind. Never have been. So I just finish the search. Feeling heavy. It was an exposed needle, a used needle, a druggie's needle. For now, those are the only thoughts in my head.

A teammate runs me down to St Thomas's Hospital for blood tests and a hepatitis jab. The prisoner must have felt some degree of remorse, because he consents to give a blood sample too. That also gets handed over to the good people at Tommy's. Then the wait.

It's days rather than weeks but, until you get the all clear, it's always there in your mind. Eventually I get the good news. I'll never make that mistake again.

*

Family aside, I would rather pass time in the company of police officers than almost anyone else. I spend a huge proportion of my waking hours with them and there is so much about them that I have grown to admire: their bravery, their kindness, their simple human decency, their occasionally questionable sense of humour, the ability they have to make the back end of a patrol car slide sideways when taking a corner at speed.

There's something about those friendships that are formed in extraordinary and often extreme circumstances. These are people who have walked where I have walked − and who understand.

There are conversations you can have with your colleagues that are difficult to have with anyone else. How can you even begin to explain the mangled mess of a car wreck, the charred remains discovered in the aftermath of a house fire or the harrowing detail of a child death, unless you're in the company of someone who has been there too? It's one of the reasons why many police officers end up in relationships with one another. Or with A&E nurses.

One of the lads on the team walks over to me in the station writing room − the space set aside for us to complete our paperwork at the end of the shift. He tells me that I've had a phone call and hands me a page from an official police memo pad. It shows the name 'Liz' and gives a central London phone number.

I don't know anyone called Liz, so assume it must be a query from a victim of crime. I pick up the nearest phone and dial the number. The voice at the other end is extremely well spoken. 'Buckingham Palace. Can I help you?'

As I mumble a hurried apology and offer something lame

about dialling the wrong number, there are muffled sounds of laughter from the other side of the room.

*

I finally get my posting as operator on the Area Car, a reward for working hard on the team on a consistent basis. Our call sign is Lima 3 and we will have first refusal on all the good calls. I've never been in a proper car chase and I can't help feeling as though I've so far missed out on one of the highlights of a policing life.

The TSG are on the ground and one of their carriers puts up a suspect vehicle on Acre Lane. The TSG – or Territorial Support Group to give them their full name – are a central Met unit, trained and equipped to deal with public disorder. When there are no marches or demonstrations going on, they deploy to London's crime hotspots in support of local officers. They usually turn up in three vans containing six or seven officers each and, today, they're with us.

The car they're following has just done a red light and they've still got it in sight. Game on. We head down Brixton Hill, anticipating that we'll catch up with them somewhere near the town hall. My hand is hovering over the car radio, ready to press transmit and take up the commentary.

We are bang on the money. As we approach the junction from the south, we see the car with the carrier coming up behind it. It does another red light. But, just as my sense of excitement is reaching a peak, the car simply pulls over, with the TSG bus right behind it. Dammit. Not only is there no chase, but some other PC is going to steal my prisoner. I jump out of the car and run forward, still hoping for some of the action. But nothing is as it seemed.

The car isn't stolen and it doesn't contain a gang of hardened criminals. Not even a petty thief. Instead, in the driving seat is a distressed husband. Curled in a semi-foetal position in the front passenger footwell is his wife and she's in the advanced stages of labour. My grumpy sense of grievance vanishes.

One of the TSG lads gets into the driver's seat of the car and we lead a three-vehicle blue-light convoy to King's. I jump out at A&E and run inside, looking for someone other than me to deliver the baby.

It's not just about crime.

*

For all the time I spend in the company of highly trained police drivers, I don't yet have a driving licence of my own. I'd had my first lesson on my seventeenth birthday, but when Dad left, it just fell by the wayside. Along with so many other things.

I'm now in my mid-twenties and it's time I got my act together. Except that I don't find the whole test-passing thing entirely straightforward. In fact, I need three attempts. My sister Annie – with just the one eye – had passed first time. My elder brother's ego is dealt a healthy blow.

Simon – one of the senior PCs on the team – sells me his old blue Rover and, something like nine years after my first driving lesson and one clutch change later, I am finally in possession of my own set of wheels.

*

I learn that, as a police officer, you're never really off duty. You never know when you might be needed. Early in my career, I had been visiting Annie in Cambridge, when I dropped round to her local supermarket for some supplies. Once inside, I heard raised voices and the sound of scuffling in a neighbouring aisle. Instinctively, I went to investigate and found a pile of bodies with an apparent shoplifter buried at the bottom of them. Store security and a number of members of the public had managed to restrain the suspect pretty effectively and he was going nowhere. Then an interesting thing happened.

I felt duty-bound to offer some assistance and so I identified myself as a police officer. As I did so, without a word and in complete unison, everyone let go of the thief. He jumped up and produced an uncapped syringe. He waved it in an arc around him, shouting, 'HIV ... HIV ...' Perhaps unsurprisingly, everyone took several steps backwards, leaving me on my own with him. And I had no option but to let him run out of the store.

Then there was the day a London bus conductor got assaulted on the lower deck of the 137. I was minding my own business upstairs when I heard the sounds of a struggle below. I made the arrest and booked him into the local custody suite.

There was the day when Winston, a kind and decent member of staff at Clapham North Tube station, got punched in the face by some lowlife passenger. It happened right in front of me. I'm not the strongest person in the world, but I managed to wedge the suspect into the space between ticket barrier and wall and hang onto him until the local uniform arrived.

The same with the oversized shoplifter at Sainsbury's on Clapham High Street, though I needed the help of the security guards to keep hold of him. Another day off interrupted.

The first occasion on which I spotted a suspect stealing car stereos outside my kitchen window, he got away. I ended up with cuts all over the back of my hand in the struggle to detain him. Second time it happened, I caught the thief.

Then there are the crashes. On one occasion, I was on the M3 on my way back to London after a visit to Mum and backed up in the traffic when I saw a belch of thick black smoke up ahead of me. A car was in flames. I leaned on the horn and headed up the hard shoulder as fast as I dared.

The car, facing the wrong way in the outside lane, was a fireball and I couldn't get anywhere near it. But it seemed as though everyone had got out in time.

So I turned my attention to the man with burns on his face, lying on the grass at the edge of the tarmac. He was conscious and appeared to have been very fortunate. He was in shock and doubtless feeling a good deal of pain, but he was going to be OK.

I stayed with him and his relatives – offering reassurance and monitoring his condition – until the uniformed patrols and paramedics arrived on scene and I was able to return to my own car and wait for the scene to clear.

You're never really off duty at all.

*

For the last couple of years, Dad has been living an itinerant life, moving from one place to another in search of a peace that seems forever beyond his reach. For now, he is living in a soulless flat just off the Commercial Road in east London. I took my sisters over there last Christmas and it was utterly miserable.

During the year I had spent commuting between school in Basingstoke and home in London, Dad and I would often head off to the cinema at the weekends. It was one of the few things I looked forward to back then.

It's a habit we renew now that he's living in town. It's a good excuse to spend some time together, while avoiding the inevitable pain and awkwardness that any kind of prolonged conversation might bring.

One evening, we meet in Leicester Square. Dad isn't in great shape – broke as well as broken. So I buy the tickets to the film and, at the end of the evening, dig into my trouser pocket to give him the money for his Tube fare back east.

And everything is the wrong way round. I continue to be more of a dad to him than he is able to be to me.

Eventually, he finds his way back to a monastery – one hidden away in a patch of beautiful Sussex woodland – and he reverts to a much simpler, more disciplined existence. I drive down to see him and I am taken by the stillness of the place, in compelling contrast to the madness of work and the relentless pace of my London existence.

At the end of each visit, there will be another painful goodbye, an echo of the first. I still love him.

*

Back at work, I'm already losing count of the dead bodies I've seen. But I've yet to confront my own mortality.

I'm guesting for a shift with one of the other response teams and I'm paired up with a driver with one hell of a story to tell. Not so long ago, he and a colleague were out on mobile patrol in Coldharbour Lane. As they were passing the junction with Rushcroft Road, they saw what they believed to be a drug deal taking place. They got out to challenge the two suspects and, as they were approaching, one of the men drew a handgun. He shot both PCs. Just like that. Officers down.

As they lay in the street, seriously wounded, the gunman came and stood over them. He fired another shot into the air in apparent celebration, before making off on the back of a moped ridden by his accomplice.

They had enough strength left to call for help on the radio and both somehow survived. The psychopath who shot them was later caught and convicted. After a lengthy period of recovery and rehabilitation, both were given their choice of posting. And both chose to return to Brixton, to the very streets where their lives had so nearly come to an end. They are men of uncommon courage.

*

The timber yard just round the corner from where I live is on fire.

Earlier this week, a black man died in the cells at Brixton Police Station and there have been protests and disorder on the streets, including acts of arson. There's a desperately sad sense of familiarity to it all.

I am back on duty the morning after the worst of it and I

can feel the tension in the air – the sense of unease, of uncertainty, of anger on all sides. But, thank God, things settle down and there's no more trouble. At least not this year.

*

I come to the end of my time at Brixton. It has been a place of great adventure. It has taught me endless things, shown me innumerable sorrows and introduced me to so many of life's lost souls. More than anything, though, it has affirmed for me that the Met is where I am meant to be, doing what I am meant to be doing. And, every now and then, I have made a difference.

V. *Sarge*

I've completed three and a half years as a PC, barely enough time to get the hang of things. So much of policing can only really be learned by doing, and experience counts for a great deal. But this is all the time I've allowed myself and it will have to do. I've got a place on something called the Accelerated Promotion Programme and that carries a certain level of expectation in terms of progress. I've passed my sergeant's exam and that means stripes on my shoulders and a move a couple of miles east, from Brixton to Peckham.

I still look far too young to be a police officer, never mind to be in charge of other police officers. I'm still the geography graduate with a plummy accent and precious little life experience. I still get spots. In truth, I'm still Johnny the Boy.

*

It's an image I do little to dispel as Mum, driving her none-too-subtle bright-yellow VW Beetle, drops me off outside the front door of Peckham nick on my first morning. I have a load of kit and nowhere to park my own car – but still.

Fortunately, I don't think anyone notices and I escape without the indignities of a maternal kiss on the forehead and a loving exhortation to play nicely with the others.

I'm taken off on a tour of the station while the team I'll be joining are having a meeting somewhere on the first floor. In my absence, one of the other sergeants lets my new colleagues know that I'll be starting with them the following day. The PCs call him 'Sompy' and he's old enough to be my dad.

As he makes reference to my three and a half years' experience, one of the PCs in the room pipes up, 'I've got a pair of trousers with more years in the job than that!' This is related back to me by Sompy, with no small amount of delight, towards the end of the day.

But the team make me welcome and I start to settle into my new role as their Permanent Custody Sergeant. It's a formal position – booking in prisoners, authorising detention, overseeing the progress of investigations – that offers some cover for my lack of confidence, both personal and professional.

As I learn my trade, I'm afforded a front-row seat for the parade of life that comes through every police cell block: the addicts and the abusers, the thieves and the tormentors, the drunks and the dealers, the men of violence and the mentally ill. All of life is here. There are the alcoholics who can't stand up. There are the junkies who promise they're off the gear. There are the depressed and suicidal in desperate need of expert medical assistance. A police cell is the very last place they need to be. There are the career criminals and the opportunist thieves. There are the non-English speakers and the much-travelled asylum seekers. There are the persistent young offenders, foul-mouthed, boundary-less and without any apparent empathy or care for the world around them. There are the rapists and the child abusers.

And there are the killers.

*

There's a PC standing in front of me in the custody suite with a battered and swollen face. He's an extraordinarily brave man. We've had a murder this evening and this lone officer has chased the suspect through a succession of back gardens, fighting with him hand to hand and hanging on desperately until the back-up arrived. Now there's a maniac safely locked up and one mightily courageous copper in need of patching up.

*

After six months based at the station, performing my custody duties, it's time to take on the role of Patrol Sergeant – out on the street, under the leadership of an inspector, supervising the PCs answering 999 calls. For sheer fulfilment, it's right up there with some of the best jobs I've ever done.

I stand in the corridor between the control room and the custody suite, looking at my watch. I'm actually disappointed that the shift is passing too quickly. I can barely keep up with the headlong adventure of it all.

*

It's an early morning in south London and I've volunteered to deliver a death message. It's not something I've ever had to do before. The deceased was only a teenager. He went round to a friend's house in Pimlico for the night, had too much to drink, lit a cigarette and fell asleep on the sofa with it still burning in his hand. He set the whole place alight and put his own flame out. Brutal and final and awful.

We've got a name and a possible address, but we're not 100 per cent sure. As I walk up the front path with two other officers, I can feel the weight of the news I'm carrying. I'm rehearsing my lines in my head.

A man opens the door and I ask a gentle question. Yes, we're in the right place. And when is a copper on the front step ever good news?

'I'm so sorry...'

I am the teller of the tale and he is the hearer of the unbearable news. The realisation comes later that this is the only conversation I will ever have with him. I invite myself in and see at least half a dozen other family members, staring at me and fearful of what is to come. Last night brought the end of one young life. This morning brings, in some respects at least, the end of theirs. My colleagues and I are unavoidably intruders on their grief.

We do what we can – cover the practicalities, offer lifts to the hospital, try to be kind. Then, just as we arrived, we step back out of their lives. And take the next call.

*

Another early turn and I go to take a crime report on a local estate. Nothing too serious, but there's a victim to reassure and to help if I can. As I venture onto the estate, I'm struck by how quiet it is and by the imposing bars that cover every window within reach. The communal doors are controlled by an entry-phone system and when I get to my victim's own front door it looks suitably forbidding. There's just a sense of isolation about the place; of a non-specific fear; of the outside world being kept at a distance.

It occurs to me that, were it not for the uniform I'm wearing and the fact that I'm there in an attempt to right a wrong, I just wouldn't be allowed in. The door opens for me because of the job I do and that seems to me to be a rare privilege. Police officers walk in the places where no one else would be permitted and in the places where no one in their right mind would choose to go.

*

Tom moves in as my new flatmate. We've known each other for years and have become great friends. We first met as teenagers on an Easter holiday camp and discovered that we had much in common, not least a deep faith, a love of life and a terrible sense of humour. He will later join Titus as a best man at my wedding. For now, he's the one due to get married in a few months and he needs to save every penny. I offer him favourable terms for the spare room.

*

Back on late turn. I'm out on patrol with my inspector when we respond to reports of some sort of disturbance on the Queens Road, up towards the Lewisham end. We're the only unit available – everyone else is busy with prisoners and other calls.

We arrive on scene, get out of the car and find the address up on the left-hand side. It's one of those big old south London townhouses, set back from the road and converted into flats. It's dark. There's a young white man standing on the front steps, about twenty-five metres away from me. Slim and dressed in scruffs, he's illuminated by a combination of street lamps in front and house lights behind. He's got a knife in his right hand. It looks like some sort of kitchen knife. And he is sawing it backwards and forwards on his own head, a curtain of blood running down his face and soaking his clothes. It reminds me of a scene from the Stephen King film *Carrie*. But the reality is far more troubling than fiction and I am faced with a picture of extraordinary desperation and misery.

I am straight onto the radio, calling for 'Urgent Assistance'. Two highly emotive words, instantaneously recognisable to police officers everywhere. It's a distress call. It's *the* distress call: the one radio transmission guaranteed to cut through the relentless background noise and prompt every available copper to drop whatever they're doing and get to the colleague who has put up the shout. It's a powerful thing.

I give the location: suspect armed with a knife. There's a reassurance in knowing that units are running, but time slows down between the call and the help getting to you.

I'm a mixture of adrenalin and caution as I draw my baton. I'm not sure what use it will be if he comes at me but, somehow, I've got a feeling he isn't going to. And, anyway, it's all I've got. I keep it hidden behind me – I don't want to antagonise him – and I venture towards the front of the house.

Keeping my distance, I try to talk to him. I get his name and attempt to calm him down, but he's highly agitated.

Something about breaking up with his girlfriend. From what I can glean, she's somewhere inside the building together with their young baby. Condition of both unknown. I'm giving updates on the radio. And the knife is still going backwards and forwards on his head and neck. Blood and more blood.

Just keep talking. He makes no movement towards me and, initially at least, seems to be responding to what I'm saying. But he flatly refuses to put down the knife. The problem is his evident and worsening condition. That and not knowing where his partner and baby are or how they are doing.

Just. Keep. Talking.

The troops arrive just as the man ducks back inside the front door, still holding the damn knife. No spare second to mess around. The firearms officers are straight in after him, no thought for their own safety, concerned only for mother and baby, and for my mess of a man.

Silence and waiting before, finally, the armed officers emerge with the bloody suspect in handcuffs. Things have turned out OK, or at least as OK as these things ever do. The man's girlfriend and baby are unharmed (in any physical sense) and he is safely in custody. No telling quite what their longer-term prospects are though – what kind of a world that child is going to be growing up in.

I see the knifeman down in the cells the next day. Cleaned up a bit and in his right mind, he remembers me from the night before. I'm certainly not going to forget him.

I head out towards the North Peckham Estate, in the days before they knocked it down. It's a place with a reputation.

I'm walking with one of the young probationers on my team, getting to know her, endeavouring to show her the ropes. In truth, I'm no older than she is and I don't feel that much more experienced. But it's important. There's a strong argument for suggesting that sergeant is the most important supervisory rank in policing. In my experience, a good skipper is absolutely indispensable. He or she sets the standards, the culture, the tone, the level of expectation and the appetite for work. There's just no substitute for high-quality frontline leadership – feet on the street, not tucked under a desk.

Early on in our tour of the local sights, a call comes out on the radio to a large disturbance on the estate. Not too many details at this stage, but the area carries the ever-present possibility of serious violence. We're only a short walk away.

As we approach the location given, we can hear them. As we round a bend on one of the service roads, we are faced with a group of at least thirty teenagers and young men running at full tilt in our direction. Their demeanour is far from innocent.

Urgent Assistance again.

I put it up on the radio instinctively, fearing that my colleague and I are about to be overrun. But, as soon as they set eyes on us, they starburst, scattering in every which direction. Just as well, because we wouldn't have stood a chance. I give futile chase as they vanish like vapour into endless rat runs and cut throughs. As the cavalry turn up, I'm tempted to feel a bit stupid, with nothing to show for my alarm call. But then I wonder what might have been.

*

It's 1997 and the England football team are in the midst of another World Cup qualifying campaign. It's Peckham's turn to supply officers for the game. I arrive at the briefing with my team of six PCs to be told that our posting this evening is to the players' tunnel. Beats standing in the car park.

The only bit of actual police work we have to do all evening is to see the team coach through the gate and into the stadium. That takes at least five minutes of our time. For the rest of the evening, there is little to do except enjoy an uninterrupted view of the match from behind the goal – and to gather players' autographs. Strictly speaking, I'm not sure that police pocketbooks are meant to be used for the signatures of England footballers, but that's the challenge I set my team. The winner will be the one with the most names. They set about their task with a degree of enthusiasm that is really rather heartening.

Towards the end of the evening, one of the youngest lads on my team approaches me. He's still in his probation, having moved down from Manchester to join the Met. He has an otherworldly expression on his face as he opens his notebook to show me the names of Gary Neville and a certain David Beckham. He is lost for words and genuinely close to tears. I'm chuckling.

The following morning, another of the PCs who was at Wembley with us bowls into parade with a big grin on his face. He announces that, last night, he shook hands with

Graeme Le Saux, the Chelsea player. He tells us that, when washing this morning, he was careful to keep his right hand outside the shower and that he now has a left hand and a Le Saux hand. I'm still chuckling.

*

Mum is diagnosed with bowel cancer.

The medics catch it early and she's admitted to St Thomas's for surgery. One location, endless associations. This is where we drove the family of the young lad who died in the house fire. This is where I once dropped by to see a former girl-friend who was working as a nurse in A&E. This is where the victims of violence arrive for their X-rays and stitches. This is where, one day, all three of my children will be born.

For now, it is where Mum's life is being saved, as the surgeons work their miracles.

*

I get a posting to the Q Car. It's the borough's plain-clothes, proactive crime posting and it's a feather in the cap.

Paul is the advanced driver behind the wheel. Don is the DC in the operator's seat. And I'm the skipper in the back. For six weeks, we are given licence to go looking for trouble not of our own making. As fate would have it, I'm not even in the car when the worst and best of that trouble come to pass.

We're at Brixton doing some paperwork and I offer to finish it off so the other two can get back out on patrol. They don't need a second invitation. They haven't been out long when they spot a car they don't like the look of. As they pull it over, the driver decamps. Don is straight after him. Paul secures the car and finds a carrier bag full of cash in the front passenger footwell.

Don catches his man, tackles him to the ground and manages to get the handcuffs on without incident. They get him back to Brixton nick and, once in the custody suite, they take him, still handcuffed, to the cells for a search. Tucked into the front of his waistband is a loaded handgun. And once again, in my mind's eye, I turn over the thoughts of what could have been.

*

Professional development is good for you, I'm told. After the best of times as a uniform sergeant at Peckham, I'm steered towards a significant new challenge – in the main CID office at Lewisham. My new team and I will be responsible for overseeing the police response to a broad range of crimes that are committed in the borough – everything from assaults to frauds to sexual offences to car crime. They call it a level transfer. This means that I am remaining in the same rank, but moving sideways – from uniform to detective work. Without any extensive record of attainment in the field, I am given responsibility for a team of reasonably experienced investigators. For a good while, they have me for breakfast.

I still look like a boy, I have a degree, I go to church, I have that posh voice. And now I'm in the company of a small group of draft dodgers who know full well that I don't have a clue what I'm doing. None of them is unpleasant or unkind, but they evidently see me as fair game. They routinely adjourn for a leisurely meal in the canteen shortly after arriving in the morning and take the rest of the day at an even pace. They suggest that it's standard procedure to pair up at the weekend and only to work half the shift each. At the end of one tour of duty, I even return to the parking bays to find that one of my colleagues has taken my own car out on enquiries. We'll put that last one down to an honest mistake.

It's an education and I discover how things work. I also work out where my boundaries are and where to draw the lines for the people I work with. I continue to learn my trade.

There's a GBH case involving a Chinese victim. He's been attacked and badly injured with a machete. The trail leads us from a nondescript corner of a south-east London housing estate to the West End dazzle of Chinatown. Worlds within worlds.

There's a rape case involving two alcoholics, a chaotic scene, the question of consent and a victim who wavers constantly between cooperation and avoidance. Getting any kind of a statement from her proves to be impossible.

There's a kidnap case involving the son of a well-to-do family who has fallen into a life of drug addiction and got himself into debt with his dealers. I manage to find the CCTV footage of them chasing him down the train tracks at New Cross Gate. And I find my way into the witness box at the Old Bailey.

*

I get a break from work and head to the South of France with Tom and Sara, his new bride. We're staying in a hotel as part of a wider group of English folk, some I know, some I don't. One evening, before dinner, I get into a conversation with a bright, articulate woman I've not met before. Inevitably, we get on to the subject of careers.

'Oh, you're a policeman...' I'm used to people showing an interest in what I do and I enjoy talking about something I'm so passionate about. Intriguingly, she asks me what I think about politics and the effect it has on frontline policing. In reality, my direct exposure to Politics (big 'P') has been limited up to now, but I know what I've seen and what I think. She seems genuinely interested and I give her an honest answer. I tell her that, in my view, politics makes policing harder rather than easier. I suggest that most politicians appear to have, at best, a limited understanding of the reality and complexity of our operational work. I don't know of any who have significant first-hand experience of what we do or who we are. The truth is that very few of them have been where I've been – or seen what I've seen. Inevitably, this has an impact on their perspectives and on their expectations. They don't seem to appreciate, for example, the fact that societal and familial problems forged over the course of multiple generations simply aren't going to be fixed overnight. Their preference seems to be for pithy headlines and swift solutions, often at the expense of something more substantial and sustainable. And I really struggle with what it all means for my job. My objections aren't ideological and certainly not partisan, they're just a matter-of-fact take on how things seem to be.

She listens patiently to what I have to say. Then she tells me that she's an MP.

*

Part way through my time at Lewisham, the public inquiry opens into the Met's handling of the investigation into the murder of Stephen Lawrence.

I joined the Met in September 1992, less than a year before Stephen was killed. The echoes of the case and the Met's handling of it will reverberate through all my years in the job. It remains hugely emotive, understandably so. And, in the middle of all that has been said and done over more than twenty years, there remains a family who have experienced loss beyond most of our imaginings. That's the realisation that stays with me more than any other.

The public inquiry is headline news every single day. I get seconded to a team at the Yard that will be drafting the Met's response to it and I watch as the debate unfolds and the accusations flow. Am I a racist? Am I corrupt? Am I incompetent? These are the charges being levelled at the organisation and every single one of us feels it in one way or another. It's a deeply unsettling time to be a Met police officer.

At least I manage to pass my inspector's exam.

VI. *Back to Blue*

I apply for a detective inspector's job at the newly formed Racial & Violent Crime Task Force, led by Deputy Assistant Commissioner John Grieve, former head of the Anti-Terrorist Branch and one of my policing heroes. An unconventional and brilliant police officer, JG can be found in his office at weekends, dressed in jeans and a Meat Loaf T-shirt, dispensing wisdom and inspiration. He is surrounded by books of every kind and possesses a passion that is infectious. I want to work for him.

As I stand in the corridor on the ninth floor of the Yard, waiting for my interview board, Steve, one of the DIs already working on the unit, walks past and whispers in my ear: 'Be passionate,' he says. Some officers have a tendency to go into interviews and leave their personality at the door. He's encouraging me not to do that. He's telling me to be myself.

I get the job.

*

The role of the Task Force is to lead a transformation in the way the Met responds to hate crime. There's no shortage of work to do. Community Safety Units – dedicated investigation teams – are introduced in every borough. JG wants to send a clear message that the Met takes hate crime seriously and the establishment of the CSUs, with specialist training for the officers posted to them, provides compelling evidence in support of the fact. He also introduces something called an Independent Advisory Group to the heart of the organisation. It is a bold and controversial move, opening the Met up to some of its sternest critics, inviting them to take a seat at the table and asking them to contribute to the process of reform. For an organisation that has been closed to external influence of this kind for the best part of 170 years, it will take some getting used to.

Other, less controversial, innovations include the progression of Family Liaison – support offered to the relatives of murder and road-crash victims – as a specific professional discipline, and the development of new policing responses to critical incidents.

In truth, the challenge is as much cultural as it is operational. Early in my time on the Task Force, I'm asked to deliver a briefing to colleagues and I describe the Stephen Lawrence Inquiry and its immediate aftermath as '*a necessary humbling*' of the Met. I'm told later that my choice of words had offended some in the room, but I stand by them. Before Stephen's murder and prior to the inquiry, the Met felt to me like something of a closed organisation – one that, on the whole, didn't seek the views of those on the outside and didn't appreciate it when they were offered. We're the police and we know what we're doing. Institutional pride and protectionism meant we didn't take too kindly to challenge. And we certainly never said sorry. The Stephen Lawrence case found us out.

*

JG puts his head round the main office door and nods at me to join him. I never need a second invitation. I'd follow him anywhere.

His car and driver are waiting out at the front of the Yard. I have no idea where we're going and I don't ask questions. I just feel honoured to spend a bit of time in the company of the great man. Ten minutes later, we pull up in front of the National Gallery in Trafalgar Square and I follow him inside. And, for the next hour or so, he leads me through a succession of grand corridors and large spaces, offering a passionate commentary on his favourite masterpieces. Fine art has never really been my thing, but I am transfixed.

So much great leadership is founded on the capacity to inspire and John has it to a remarkable degree. The last hour has had nothing to do with the day job, but I'm ready to run further and harder for him than ever before. My regard for him will continue to grow in the coming months and any appreciation for art that I develop later in life will be because of him.

*

Hendon is home to both recruit and detective training. I've been asked to deliver the regular Racial & Violent Crime Task Force input on the Senior Investigating Officers' course.

These are the men and women charged with leading murder investigations. And so I find myself in a classroom full of experienced senior detectives (with no experience as an SIO myself) talking about stuff that is new to all of us. I try to explain, for instance, that utilising independent advice – the non-police perspectives of those who might previously have been regarded as critics of policing – in a murder investigation is not some futile exercise in political correctness, but that it will actually enable us to do a better job than would otherwise have been possible.

Things are fairly lively at first, with plenty of opposition in the room and a certain degree of cynicism. There's even a bit of outright hostility from some quarters. But over time, as I return for subsequent courses, the SIOs begin to tell the stories themselves. I no longer need to persuade them – they have seen it work first hand.

We will always do our job better working with partners and communities than we ever would by operating in isolation. To borrow a phrase from Martin Luther King, we are not independent, we are interdependent. The Met has shown that it can change. Just as well, given the fact that we're far from done.

*

Love. It's been a complete mystery to me for so much of my life, but it finds me in the end.

A few years back, I was a guest at a wedding in south-east England. My cousin Sonia was marrying Jim, a young doctor from North Yorkshire, and they made for a handsome and happy couple. It was a blazing summer's day in Sevenoaks, with large clumps of wild flowers arranged in an assortment of old welly boots, lining the path to the church door. The bride was, of course, stunning. But, truth be told, I paid her rather less attention than I ought to have done.

The problem was Jim's sister. There she was, among the bridesmaids, all blue dress and blonde hair and beauty, and when she stood and sang a perfect, crystalline solo during the signing of the register, I was mesmerised.

She seemed to be known to everyone by the nickname Bear and she had me before hello. But I would have to concede that my wide-eyed appreciation wasn't entirely reciprocated. In fact, she completely blanked me. For the entire day.

Looking back, it might have had something to do with my appearance. I was sporting a grade-four haircut – grade two round the back and sides – and a dreadful, thigh-length blue-and-white striped jacket that I'd bought in the Kings Road and had assumed was the height of fashion. With the benefit of hindsight, I realise that I actually looked like a deckchair. Still, by way of some consolation, I suppose I didn't leave her with a bad impression of me. I succeeded in leaving no impression at all.

*

Over time, thoughts of the girl in the blue dress are set aside as the years – and the relationships – meander on. I turn thirty in early 2000 and experience a crisis of sorts. A number of my close friends, Tom among them, have got married and some of them have started having children. Work is good, but I feel as though the rest of life is leaving me behind. Spring that year plays host to a uniquely painful break-up and, during the summer, I retreat to the Rockies in North America in search of some elusive peace.

But then comes the autumn and a definite changing of the seasons.

*

One evening in September, my aunt – Sonia's mum – rings and mentions that Jim's sister is now living in Fulham. Her name is Rowan. My church is in that neck of the woods and my aunt wonders whether I might take her along. I do the chivalrous thing and tell her that she is welcome to pass my number on. It's been so long since the wedding and I am still so bruised by the experience of my last relationship that I don't make any connection. My mind is just elsewhere.

I hear nothing and think no more of it, until a few days later when I'm chatting with my two sisters and they mention Rowan and the Sevenoaks wedding of a few years before. They make the connection for me. This Rowan is that Bear. *That bridesmaid.*

With undignified haste, I ring my aunt back and get Bear's phone number. And Rowan comes to church. Within a couple of weeks, we're going out. And she is the best thing that has ever happened to me.

*

For so much of my life, I have been afraid, most especially of people and the damage they can do to you. I learned it in childhood, I confirmed it when Dad left and I reaffirmed it every time another relationship went south. It was almost entirely subconscious, but the consequences were very real. And it is no way to live.

C. S. Lewis put it so perfectly in his book *The Four Loves*:

There is no safe investment. To love at all is to be vulnerable. Love anything and your heart will certainly be wrung
and possibly be broken. If you want to make sure of keeping it intact, you must give your heart to no one, not even
to an animal. Wrap it carefully around with hobbies and
little luxuries; avoid all entanglements; lock it up safe in
the casket or coffin of your selfishness. But in that casket –
safe, dark, motionless, airless – it will change. It will not be
broken; it will become unbreakable...

And then I met Bear.

Time to move on from the Yard. It's difficult to walk past the
front of the building without seeing someone having their
photo taken underneath the iconic triangular sign. Mention
Scotland Yard to any number of people from overseas and it
becomes clear immediately that British policing has a global
reputation that is second to none. Every day, law enforcement officers from all over the world head to the Yard for
assistance and guidance and training. Every day, Met officers
can be found on every continent, supporting investigations,
advising governments, teaching locals. The rest of the world
thinks pretty highly of us: of our expertise and achievements,
of the precious notion of policing by consent; of the fact that
we remain a largely unarmed service (an almost unbelievable reality for many observers). The Met needs to get better
at what it does. Much, much better. But we also need to be

grateful for what we have. I am proud of who I am. I am proud to be a police officer.

*

After almost two years as a DI, I make a decision that is more heart than head. Remaining an inspector, I go back to a uniform role. I know that I'm never going to be the world's greatest detective and, if I'm honest, I miss the frontline – the immediacy of the challenge, the responsibility of being among the first on scene, the chatter of the parade room, the blues and twos.

There are vacancies at Fulham in west London and I jump at the chance. My church is in the neighbourhood and Bear lives a few hundred yards down the road from the station. It's not the busiest posting in London, but there will be no shortage of challenges.

I take on a team of twenty-five PCs and four sergeants. They're a good bunch: most work hard, most care about the public we serve and most are good company. The best times will be after hours, when the senior management and the office dwellers have gone home and it's just us: a thin blue line with a willingness to respond to anything.

As ever, I look younger than I am. Certainly too young to be an inspector. As I settle into my new posting, I catch officers who've not met me before staring at my face, studying the pips on my shoulders and looking quizzical.

During the first week, I ask one of the Neighbourhood Officers – Home Beats in old money – to take me out for a wander and a look at some of the faces and places in the locality. We visit two separate housing estates and, speaking with local people along the way, have pretty much the exact same conversation in both places. The Home Beat introduces me to two groups of local residents and they all want to talk to me about the behaviour of certain young people in their neighbourhoods. On both estates, I am given the name (a different one in each place) of a teenager who has gone off the rails. And we aren't talking just about simple anti-social behaviour, we're discussing the beginnings of serious criminality.

The nub of both conversations goes something like this: 'We could always tell he was a wrong 'un – right from the age of four or five. Whenever there was trouble, he was involved. And look at him now . . .'

They are telling me that, for ten years or more, they have been predicting the outcome of each particular story. Talk about self-fulfilling prophecies. The world just stood by, wringing its hands and saying, 'I told you so.'

*

Adrian is the senior sergeant on the team. A good man and good at his job, over the years he becomes a remarkable friend to me. But not every sergeant on the team shares his appetite for work. One of them gives every appearance of just being plain lazy. I hear a whisper that, on nights, this particular individual likes to disappear and sleep the shift away in some quiet corner of the nick, while everyone else is answering calls and getting stuck in. So I decide to go looking for him. I've never been one to seek out confrontation, but if the rumours are true, he's completely out of order.

I start on the ground floor and, room by room, work my

way up through the building. As I get to the top floor, the doors of the lift open next to me and Adrian steps out. We almost bump into one another. We exchange a knowing glance and pick a different corridor each. Loyal to a fault and trying to keep a colleague out of trouble, he's trying to find the sleeping skipper before I do. If I get there first, some form of discipline for the offender will be inevitable. But I draw a blank. So does Adrian. Neither of us can find the so-and-so anywhere. However, I know now the kind of person he is, and I know that I can't trust him. Unlike Adrian, with whom I will share many an adventure, many a pint and endless bad jokes.

*

I'm the late turn Duty Officer, which means I'm leading the team of PCs and sergeants who are responding to the emergency calls. In the middle of the afternoon, they take a call from a concerned woman who has asked to meet police on the edge of the estate just next to South Park. I'm available and go to join them at the location.

We meet a woman in her forties who is visibly concerned about the well-being of her daughter. She explains that her daughter has been living with a young man on the estate and suggests that she is being abused. She believes her daughter wants to get out, but she is too afraid to do so. It's a familiar story. Domestic violence comes in many forms but, invariably, you find an abuser who is controlling, manipulative and capable of extreme violence.

Leaving mum in her car, we head up to the address on the first floor of the block and knock on the front door. It's answered by a white man wearing a vest and tracksuit bottoms. I take an instant dislike to him, with his paunch and his glare. We explain why we're there and ask to come in. There's a young woman in the sitting room. She looks tired and drawn. Two of the PCs speak to her out of his earshot. She doesn't immediately disclose that any offences have been committed against her, but she does want to leave. I'm glad. The dynamics of abusive relationships can be hugely complex and what might seem to an outsider to be the obvious course of action can be anything but to someone trapped on the inside.

As we lead her quietly away, the man in the vest decides to take centre stage. He climbs over the balustrade on the communal balcony and threatens to jump if she leaves him. It's a grotesque and desperate attempt to exert power over a vulnerable victim and there's a part of me thinking, 'Just do us all a favour and let go.' But the better part takes over and we concentrate on getting her back to her mum. He soon gives up on his appalling display and retreats indoors. I'm struggling to feel anything other than utter contempt for him.

We get an endless stream of domestic-violence calls. Every team on every shift in every part of the country is answering them. Each is a potential murder. Each is a potential rape. Each is a potential GBH. None of them is simple or straightforward. And it remains the greatest cause of harm in society.

*

Once a year, we are invited to play a cricket match at the Hurlingham, an exclusive and very smart private sports club down by the Thames. The facilities are pristine and the PCs challenge the rest of the ranks to a limited overs game. Standards are variable at best, but it's a break from the headlong rush and the cream teas are in a class of their own. This year, Mr Wills – our highly respected Borough Commander – has been persuaded to join us for the afternoon. It is he who obliges us with the defining image of the day.

It's our turn to field and the boss is standing midway between wicket and boundary. Suddenly and without any warning, he lets out a yelp and drops his trousers to his ankles. I watch with complete delight as he dances from foot to foot in his all-too-brief underwear, trying to escape the bee that had just flown up his trouser leg. It is a sight infinitely more memorable than any of the sport played that day. It is also, I suspect, a low point in his distinguished career.

*

Another late turn and I'm guesting as Duty Officer on another team. I know the faces of most of the officers, but not many of the names. I take the chance to catch up with some paperwork while keeping one ear on the radio. As evening draws in, the working channel crackles into life as one of our IRV crews report that they're chasing a Range Rover down the Cromwell Road towards Knightsbridge. An IRV is a standard response car, equipped with blue lights and sirens.

There's nothing like a vehicle pursuit to grab the attention. But something goes badly wrong and there are calls for help. I race to the scene.

I see the suspect vehicle dumped in a front garden and

the IRV stationary at an angle in the middle of the road with the front passenger door open. As I get closer, I can see the figure of a PC lying half in and half out of the car. I get a breathless update from a colleague as I run straight to him.

The Range Rover had pulled to a standstill in the middle of the road. As the IRV operator had jumped out to deal with the situation, the suspect vehicle had gone into a sudden high-speed reverse, ramming the nearside of the police car and crushing the PC between door frame and chassis.

The driver of the Range Rover has decamped and, for now, I don't give him a second thought. I climb into the driver's side of the IRV and cradle the fallen officer's head in my hands. He appears to be very seriously injured. He seems to be drifting in and out of consciousness and I speak gently and insistently, telling him to stay with us. As colleagues from other teams begin the manhunt for the suspect, we are surrounded by the officer's friends. The concern is palpable and it occurs to me that he might die in our arms.

After what seems an eternity, the ambulance crew arrive and I watch as they cut his uniform trousers off and move him slowly onto a stretcher. We're still talking to him, pleading and reassuring. As the ambulance doors close and the blue lights fade towards the nearest A&E, I call Bear. I'm shaken and I want to hear her voice. I ask her to pray and I say a quiet prayer of my own.

There's a grim feeling among his team as we hand the scene over to officers from Kensington & Chelsea – our neighbouring borough and the place where the chase ended up.

Later that night, we get the first news that he's going to be OK. He's had better days, but he's going to be OK. Then comes the really astonishing part. Despite some very severe bruising, he hasn't broken a single bone in his body.

It seems impossible to me. I was there at the scene. I saw the angle that he was lying at. I saw the state he was in. I saw the expressions on the faces of his colleagues. I watched the care with which the paramedics treated him. And it seems unbelievable that he should be in one piece. But he is.

I know I'm not the only officer present that day who wonders whether we were witness to some sort of miracle.

*

Nights. Whenever I'm out and about and the radio is quiet, I try to take the opportunity to stop and talk to people in the street. More often than not, I chat to the groups of youngsters who are more inclined than most to be mistrustful of the police. It works both ways of course. They tend to have fixed views about us and we hold to certain stereotypes about them. The misunderstandings and suspicions persist, but it's better to build bridges than walls and it's always good to talk. I genuinely enjoy their company and I want to give them the chance to see beyond the uniform.

On this particular occasion, I'm on my own in a marked car. It's about midnight when I see a fairly large group of young people standing on Fulham Broadway. They're not doing anything mischievous, but it is pretty late and it would be remiss of me not to have a word.

As I pull up, they see the car and, as one, begin to walk away. No one is running and they don't seem to have anything to hide, it's just very evident that they have no interest whatsoever in being hassled and patronised by another copper. But I've spoken to one or two of the teenage boys in the group before and they look over and recognise me. The whole group stops, turns round and comes back. And we pass the time of day (or night) talking about not much at all. But the conversation matters.

*

Bear and I spend as much time together as we can. Occasionally, on a weekday evening or when I'm on duty at the weekend, I call round to her place in full uniform. It certainly makes an impression on her housemates.

When I'm on nights, she comes to stay at the flat. I cook her an evening meal before heading out to work. We have breakfast together when I get back in the morning and she listens to my stories. I love coming home to her.

*

I'm at work, changed and ready to go, about half an hour before another night shift is due to begin. I'm in the inspectors' office, talking through the handover with my late-turn counterpart, when a call comes in concerning a possible shooting on the North End Road. I tell my colleague that I'll take it and head straight out of the door. There's a car ready in the yard and I jump in the back. A minute or two later, we pull up outside the Lighthouse Fish Bar.

It's no hoax. The owner of the takeaway is lying on the floor among the tables and chairs, with a serious shotgun wound to his stomach. The good news is that he's conscious and talking. We let the paramedics get on with the job of saving him as the PCs click into gear: cordons, scene preservation, local witness enquiries – all the requirements of that first, critical hour. My role is to coordinate everything that's happening and they do their jobs well. To provide evidential continuity, one of the PCs goes to hospital with the victim.

The dust begins to settle. Time to catch our breath and work out what we know. The Shootings Team are on the way – I've already spoken to them on the phone – and I head back to the station to chat to Ang, the Night Duty DI. We already have intelligence coming through and, pretty swiftly, we have the name of a possible suspect.

The rest of the night hurtles past. The faster we act, the better our chances of recovering critical evidence. Ang leads the investigators while I make a phone call and wake the chief superintendent from the neighbouring borough, the location of our suspect's home address. I need to get his authority for a pre-planned firearms operation on his ground. Someone else wakes a magistrate to get the warrant signed and we all get ready to move.

Everyone assembles at Fulham: me and my team, Ang and the local Night Duty CID, the investigators from the Shootings Team and several Trojan units. 'Trojan' is the call sign for the Met's Armed Response Vehicles (ARVs). The vast majority of us remain unarmed, but Trojan are always there when we need them. They are highly trained and among the most professional police officers I have ever worked with. They respond to thousands of the most serious calls every year, but only ever fire their weapons on a tiny handful of occasions. They take extraordinary personal risks to keep the rest of us safe and they have my unfailing admiration and appreciation.

After a detailed briefing, we drive in convoy across the border to Kensington & Chelsea and form up at the top end of the Kings Road, about a hundred yards from the target address. Last whispered instructions and the armed officers move in. Radio silence and another quiet prayer. Then, from a safe distance, the muffled thud of a door going in and the repeated shouts of 'Armed Police'.

No sounds of gunfire.

The message comes through on the radio: 'Suspect detained.'

And we can all move forward. One victim in hospital. One suspect in custody. One knackered but happy inspector heading home for some kip.

*

Nights again and I'm last man standing out on patrol. Everyone else is in with prisoners or otherwise off the road. We receive a call to shots fired. The location given is the side street next to McDonald's on the North End Road. I can't be more than 800 yards away. Just one of those coincidences. Big, deep breath. If not me, then who?

I park the car on the main road and walk the last bit. Cautiously. Hesitantly. I can't hear anything, but you just never know what you're going to find. I put my head round the corner and see a group of armed men encircling a saloon car that's parked at an unusual angle across the middle of the road.

A moment later, I am able to relax. They're the good guys,

members of one of the Met's armed surveillance teams, targeting guns and drugs on the streets of London. They ought to have told us they were going to be on our ground, but I'm too relieved to be annoyed.

They've put in a hard stop on a suspect vehicle they've been following and the shots reported by members of the public were Hatton Rounds being fired into the tyres of the car to stop it going anywhere. We exchange professional pleasantries and I notice one of the bad guys in particular. I notice him because he's just a kid. Now he's in handcuffs, vomiting over someone's front wall, absolutely terrified. How did he get involved in something this serious? He's somebody's child.

*

The firearms incidents keep coming. Early turn. Another infernal alarm sounding by my bed at stupid o'clock in the morning. I'm covering the whole borough today and, for the first seven hours of the shift, nothing much happens. I'm starting to think about wending my weary way home (I'm cooking supper for Bear later on) when my reverie is interrupted by the insistence of my radio.

Possible armed siege in Shepherd's Bush.

Bailiffs have visited a flat just off the Green and the occupant has barricaded himself inside. He's shouted to responding police officers that he's armed with a gun. There's an additional suggestion that he might have a hostage trapped in there with him.

This is big.

I get a Fast Car run to the scene and I'm there as the whole world begins to turn up: TSG, ARVs, negotiators and the rest. It's my first experience of anything on this scale. And, as the local Duty Officer, I'm supposed to be in charge.

I ring Bear to tell her that I'm going to be late.

The surrounding streets are locked down as the specialists begin to deploy around me. Their team leaders come to me for guidance and direction – and I look to them for the same. The plan is simple – contain and negotiate. No need for it to be any more complicated than that. We are here to save lives.

The hostage team set themselves up in the front room of a house down the street from the target premises. Sensing my inexperience, their team leader invites me in and talks me through the set-up and the plan. I'm impressed. Maybe I could be a negotiator one day.

Then the Borough Commander turns up (the one with the bee up his trouser leg) and I know for sure that things are serious. He's a good man and good leader. It would be the easiest thing in the world for him to step in and take over, but he takes a back seat and lets me find my feet. He's there if I need him, but trusts me to crack on. I'm grateful.

That said, there will be moments in the next few hours that feel pretty overwhelming. At one point, I pause in the middle of the road, in a break between endless urgent conversations, and find my lips silently mouthing a confession. 'I don't have the faintest idea what I'm doing.' But I'm surrounded by brilliant people who know and understand what's needed. I lean on them. I listen to them. And, between us, we make good decisions. We settle in for as long as this is going to take.

Someone arrives with a mobile command vehicle – word

is obviously getting round – and I become the proud posses-
sor of an office on wheels. Then it's the turn of Teapot 1 – the
Met's mobile catering van – to appear and, with it, an endless
supply of hot cuppas and sausage rolls for the gathering band
of officers. We could be here for some time and it's important
to keep people refuelled and ready.

It's not just us, of course. We're only a few hundred yards
down the road from the BBC in White City and it doesn't
take long for the press to arrive at the cordons.

Every half hour, on the half hour, I gather the team leaders
back together. Any updates? Any need to vary the plan? All
contingencies in place?

I ring Bear to say that I'm going to be even later.

The Level 1 firearms team – specially trained and equipped
to respond to incidents such as this one – turn up at the
rendezvous point. It's the first time I've encountered them
for real. They arrive in a convoy of unmarked cars, with a
van bringing up the rear. Sitting in their vehicles, they are a
procession of non-descript T-shirts, blank expressions and
obligatory shades. I watch, fascinated, as they kit up in the
street in front of me. Overalls are unknotted from waists and
pulled up over gym-honed shoulders. Then comes the hardware – assorted firearms strapped to legs and armoured vests
and all manner of spare magazines and accessories fixed to
body-worn harnesses. As the man in front of me turns to
face away from me, I see an axe velcroed to the small of his
back. Blimey, I'm glad they're on my side.

The watching and waiting continues. Patience needed.
I've been on duty for about fifteen hours now, fuelled and

sustained by adrenalin and the sense of proper adventure. Then, just as I'm beginning the process of handing over command to a night-duty colleague, I hear that the officers who have been outside the target address for the last few hours have somehow managed to persuade the suspect to surrender. It's all over.

And we discover that there was no gun and no hostage. But you can never know these things until the end. And the end can sometimes be so very different. This time round, though, it's back slaps all round.

I arrived at Shepherd's Bush earlier today as a rookie uniform inspector with no experience of anything like this. I slip away quietly at the end of it all having worked two full shifts in a single day and having been caught up in a masterclass delivered by the Met's finest.

Bear is waiting with a meal at home and, as I slide into a hot bath, I am exhausted and elated in equal measure. To my mind, there's no other job that comes remotely close to this one.

*

A couple of days later, an email from the Borough Commander pops up in my inbox. That hasn't happened to me before. In his message, he tells me that he wants to award me a commendation: 'For leadership of the highest calibre during a complex siege'. I feel like the king of the world.

*

I still haven't ever been in a proper vehicle pursuit and that fact remains a source of some regret. But things might be about to change. I'm out with one of the PCs on nights and he's driving us round the back streets near Baron's Court Tube. We're heading south down Palliser Road towards Queens Club when we take a slow left turn into Barton Road. And there, immediately in front of us, is a white Transit with two young suspects lifting a moped into the open side door. Thefts of this sort are a fairly frequent crime in these parts, but you could patrol the neighbourhood for months without ever coming across one directly. Our luck is in.

As soon as they see us, the two lads drop the bike and throw themselves into the van. Plenty of revs and it's off.

This is it. This, finally, is my moment.

The van accelerates and I reach for the mainset radio: 'MP... MP... Foxtrot Foxtrot One... Active Message...' Nothing. I try again: 'MP... MP... Foxtrot Foxtrot One... Active Message...' The sodding thing is broken. We are approximately five seconds into the chase.

I turn my attention to my personal radio only to find that Chris, the acting sergeant in the control room, is holding forth at great length on a subject of no importance whatsoever. I can't get in with the commentary I've been waiting my whole career to deliver without pressing my emergency button and cutting him off. But, before I can think about doing that, the van takes a sharp left into Baron's Court Road. And then it slams to a stop. We are about ten seconds in.

Four occupants starburst and I'm out and after them. Fleetingly, it strikes me that I have just taken part in the shortest car chase in the history of the Metropolitan Police. It was hardly worth the wait. But my regrets are, of necessity, set aside to focus on sprinting. We go past the Tube station and across the busy A4, where the suspects disappear over the wall of a local college. Fortunately, Chris has finally stopped talking on the radio and there are plenty of other units on the way. We manage to catch them all, including the one who, inexplicably, stayed hiding inside the Transit.

I tell myself that my virtuoso performance on the mainset – broadcast to a Met-wide audience – will just have to wait for another day. Part of the thrill of the chase is to be found in the fact that everyone else knows it's happening.

*

Guns and more guns.

Gun crime is actually fairly rare, particularly in this part of west London, but I seem to be involved in a run of cases.

The southern boundary to our patch is located halfway across Wandsworth Bridge, the point at which our neighbouring borough takes over. Calls come through in the middle of the night to a shooting on their side of the river. We're close by and we offer to help out.

The victim is in a car on the big roundabout at the bottom of Trinity Road. He's been shot in the head at point-blank range, by an unknown assailant who has long since fled the scene. Goodness knows what it was all about. Drug rivalries or debts, I suspect. But the footnote to this round of insanity is that the victim survives. He's been shot with homemade ammunition and it's of poor enough quality to have disintegrated on impact with his skull. He's not well, but he's not dead.

Bad people frequently find proper stuff hard to come by, so they make their own. A gentle nudge here to folk across the pond. Gun control works. Which is just as well, given our capacity for senselessness.

*

I'm speaking to the victim of another shooting in Charing Cross Hospital. At least, I'm trying to. He's lying there with gunshot wounds, guarded by armed officers, and he's saying nothing. Not a word.

I try telling him that, whether he likes me or not, whether he trusts the police or not, whether he generally gives a damn of any kind, there's a gunman out there somewhere and we have innocent lives to protect. I might as well be talking to the wall, confounded by some kind of west London *omertà*.

*

Most police officers like a drink from time to time, but you're unlikely to find the fabled half-empty bottle of whisky in the DI's bottom drawer. The alcohol tends to flow off-duty these days. For most officers, it's an opportunity to unwind after a long shift. For some, it's a means of dulling the senses at the end of a particularly testing day or night at work.

I'm a hopeless drinker, with no real capacity for the stuff. Two or three pints are about as much as I can manage, but I love the company of coppers and I'm happy for them to consume my share. Some of the team like to go for a jar or two at Spitalfields Market after a night shift and, after much persuasion, I agree to join them one morning. We drink beer at the wrong end of the day, eat bacon sandwiches and laugh ourselves senseless, before I weave my way home in a contented daze. I manage not to oversleep for that evening's shift.

＊

Time to go to shield training. In addition to the full-time expertise of the TSG, a number of local officers from boroughs are also trained to deal with riots and other forms of public disorder. We're effectively a reserve and we undertake the training in addition to our normal duties.

The Met has a large, purpose-built training facility in Hounslow. It has its own network of streets, complete with mock storefronts and alleyways, providing a safe environment for some dangerous professional development. From all that I've heard, the experience of having wooden bricks and petrol bombs thrown at you for two days straight can actually be a whole lot of fun.

Hounslow is where I'm headed for the next forty-eight hours, together with Adrian and some of the Fulham PCs. However, no sooner have we arrived at the site than we are told that the boiler in the canteen has blown up and our sessions have been cancelled.

Adrian takes one look at me and says, 'Let's get a plane.' He's been taking flying lessons and, having recently gained his licence, all he now wants to do is find the nearest stretch of runway and a plane he can borrow. Well, I don't have any other plans. Stuey, one of the PCs on our team and a qualified glider pilot, comes along for the ride.

After the shortish drive to Fairoaks and some cursory pre-flight checks, I fold myself into the back of the four-seat tin can that Adrian has booked out and we taxi to the runway. The mission is Southend and back. The prize is a visit to McDonald's before the return journey.

The first leg is uneventfully enjoyable – just spectacular views and the company of good friends. But on the way back we pass over Epsom racecourse in west London. Adrian and Stuey, occupying the two front seats, look at one another and the challenge is issued. *Fly the course.*

At however many thousand feet, the objective appears to be to follow every twist and bend of a track designed for thoroughbred racehorses that have a tighter turning circle than your average light aircraft. The newly qualified pilot and the glider jockey think this is a splendid idea. The passenger in the back is not consulted.

And they're off.

As they sit in the front seats, throwing the plane this way and that and cackling like a pair of characters from a Larson cartoon, I start to feel less well. I attempt to maintain a measure of dignity – I am, after all, the ranking officer on board – but it's no good. I'm about to throw up over the pair of them.

'I'm feeling a bit queasy,' I say quietly.

They think this is hilarious, but take pity on me and ease off the rudder. I just about manage to hang on to the contents of my stomach, but I'm still feeling absolutely wretched when we land back at Fairoaks. And, to think, I could have spent the entire afternoon on fire at Hounslow if the boiler hadn't packed up.

For the first time, I get to police football matches at QPR, Fulham and Chelsea. Monitoring the behaviour of fans provides a fascinating study in human behaviour and not always in a good way. Most supporters are there simply to enjoy the game, but some go through a strange metamorphosis as they approach the ground. I call it 'the turnstile transformation' – when otherwise perfectly reasonable, sensible, adult human beings pull on their club colours and turn themselves into one-eyed, fouled-mouthed, hate-filled morons. They are very much the minority, but the numbers are sufficient to leave you tempted to despair at humanity.

I'm on duty today for a Chelsea v. Manchester United Premier League fixture. The history between the two clubs or, more specifically, between the two sets of supporters, means that it has been designated as a 'Category C' match. This means that we have intelligence to suggest the potential for trouble.

The game itself passes peacefully enough but we're not done yet. As the away fans exit the stadium, we form a cordon – a protective bubble – around them. The plan is to walk with them eastwards down the Fulham Road and put them directly onto the Tube at Earl's Court, away from the crowds on the Broadway. Mounted officers accompany us along the chosen route. We are about four hundred yards down the road when someone throws a punch. I don't see who. But it comes from outside the cordon and connects with a Man United fan a few feet away from me. I watch as, in seeming slow motion, he goes down, falling under the legs of one of the larger horses. Animal and rider try desperately to avoid him but I stand there, powerless, as hoof makes contact with skull.

Heads bleed a lot. He survives the encounter, but he's going to need an awful lot of stitches. And all for what?

Last game of the season at Loftus Road, home of Queens Park Rangers. The local fans have a reputation for running onto the pitch at the end of the final fixture and their intentions towards opposing supporters are not always honourable.

My immediate boss and the Match Commander for the day, Mick Moody, makes his view clear: 'Once they're past the halfway line, they're not there to say hello.'

Sure enough, as the referee's whistle goes, hundreds of them clamber over the advertising hoardings and start to advance towards the away end. We're ready for them.

I lead a team of officers in protective public order kit onto the playing area and we're joined by the full might of Mounted Branch – horses as big as houses. And we march the miscreants all the way back to their seats.

One–nil to the Old Bill.

My public order duties extend beyond the football.

I'm standing in full riot gear in Parliament Square. The hunt protests are happening and I'm in charge of the group of officers stationed immediately in front of the St Stephens entrance to the Palace of Westminster. There are the pro-hunt people and the anti-hunt people and everyone seems to be angry with someone.

We pick up the rumour that some of them are planning to storm the main Parliament building. Our job is to stop them. My briefing to the team is a simple one: 'No one gets through.'

The carriers line up across the road and we fill the gaps in between them – shields out and visors down. They try but they don't get past. It's all over the papers the following day. Once again – as is so often the case with policing – we are the lead item on the news.

*

Bear is wonderful. Tom reckons I should ask her to marry me. The thought is appealing and overwhelming in equal measure.

*

It's strange how each of the senses seems to possess a memory of its own. I'm back on nights with the team and we've been called to a ground-floor maisonette in one of the side streets off the New Kings Road. The young guy who lives there – in his late twenties, I suppose – has been seriously ill for some time and now he isn't answering his door. Concerned friends have raised the alarm. My team have forced their way in by the time I get there.

I step inside and it hits me.

He hasn't been dead for that long, but the smell is almost completely overwhelming. The heating's on full and it has hastened the decaying process. I try to breathe through my mouth rather than my nose but still find myself retching.

Later, as I savour the fresh air back out in the street, I am struck by the fact that here I am again in the final resting place of someone who died on their own. He lived in a decent place and didn't seem to be wanting in any material sense. He had friends who called us when they couldn't get hold of him. But no one was with him when that last moment came. Not for the first time, it strikes me that it just shouldn't be so.

For years afterwards, at the most unexpected moments, I will catch the remembrance of that smell in my nostrils.

*

More death.

It's the middle of the afternoon and we've been called to a ground-floor flat in a side street off the Fulham Palace Road. The male occupant hasn't been seen for a while – and so the call comes our way. We force entry.

He's been lying face down on the floor for a good while and his body has begun to rot away. As we try to move him to look for any injuries, he begins to come apart in our hands. Like a chicken from the hot counter. Sometimes you need a really strong stomach.

As I later step back out of the front door, the lady from one of the adjoining houses leans over the front wall and proudly shows me her grand-looking invitation to the wedding of Hollywood Royalty, Michael Douglas and Catherine Zeta-Jones. She tells me that Catherine used to live round here. She doesn't know about the fate of her other neighbour – the disintegrating man next door – and I haven't the heart to tell her.

*

I'm back on night duty again. London is different after dark. Away from the noise and neon of the West End and the head-down hustle of late-finishing commuters going home – as most people are settling down at the end of the day – the capital has a tendency to reveal its sad stories. Police officers – and feral foxes – are often the only witnesses to them.

We've been contacted by Social Services about a child at risk – a young girl of about ten, living with her mum in a block of flats up the North End Road. The concern is her mum's mental health, which has deteriorated to such an extent that a Court Order has been obtained to take the child into protection. Given the hour of the night, it falls to us to knock on the door. I take a couple of the team with me. It's approaching midnight. The mum lets us in and you can tell straight away that she's not well: her eyes, her mannerisms, the things she's saying.

I tiptoe into the sleeping girl's bedroom, not wanting to alarm her. I keep my uniform hat on in the hope that this might reassure her and I gently call her name. She wakes and is completely calm. I explain that we need to take her to stay with someone else and she seems to take it all in her stride. Perhaps this isn't the first time. And I try to explain it all to her mum who is, unsurprisingly, becoming increasingly agitated. I send my two colleagues down to the car with her daughter and do my best to calm her. I end up bear hugging her as, wild-eyed and wailing, she tries to follow them downstairs. There's no manual for this and it's just awful.

I manage to extricate myself without injury and close the front door behind me. But I leave a broken life alone on the other side. I feel a deep sense of unease. Perhaps I should call an ambulance for her, but then what? I have no power to detain her inside her own home and she's offered no indication that she might be at immediate risk of harming herself. But she is seriously unwell and I am left only with questions.

Did we do the right thing? We had the necessary legal authority and we acted with entirely honourable intentions, but was it *right*? Was it even a job for the police? Why hadn't the mental-health and child-protection professionals dealt with it yesterday or waited until the morning? Perhaps it's just easier to let us take the strain. I am consoled only by the fact that the young girl is safe, for now at least. I hope and pray that, one day, her mum will be too.

*

I'm single crewed in a car on another night shift and I'm looking to do my bit. Leading by example, and all that. One of the things about Fulham is that, after about two in the morning, it's more or less completely deserted. And anyone out and about at that time is invariably lost, drunk or up to no good.

I see the man walking down Parsons Green Lane, towards the Green itself. I find out later that his name is John. Older-looking white bloke, wiry build, dressed in scruffy clothes. And he just isn't right. Even for a man of my limited thief-taking instincts, it doesn't take too much to work out that he needs speaking to. So I stop the car and get out. I do everything by the book, introducing myself and explaining my suspicions. I start to search him and find gloves and a screwdriver in the first pocket I look in.

I don't know if you've ever been punched full in the face. I don't even see it coming. He just stands and stares at me as I stumble back shouting out in a mixture of anger and shock, my lip split open and my pressed white shirt rapidly turning a shade of crimson. This job can really hurt sometimes.

Onto the radio. *Urgent Assistance.*

And John's on his toes, running down the road as adrenalin gets the better of common sense and I take off after him. Back on the radio. *Chasing suspects. Parsons Green Lane towards the New Kings Road.*

That's when he makes his mistake. He heads down the Mews next to the car showroom and I know it's a dead end. I'm still on my own and, had I been thinking clearly, I might have waited for the help to arrive. But I'm not, and I don't. Enter the milkman.

In a completely deserted corner of west London, at some unearthly hour of the morning, halfway down a no-through road, there he is. Sitting in his milk float, minding his own business. I must look a right state when he sees me but, without any hesitation, he jumps out and joins in the chase. Suddenly I'm not on my own any more.

By this time, John has worked out that he has nowhere to go and stops in the middle of the cobbled pathway. He reaches down the front of his trousers, pulls out a full-length set of bolt croppers and throws them down onto the ground in front of him. Goodness only knows how he managed to run with those in his pants, but it might go some way towards explaining the ease with which I have been able to keep up. Quick as anything, the milkman picks them up and, for the briefest of moments, I actually think he's going to lamp my suspect with them. He doesn't. In the end, it's a series of slightly more conventional baton strikes to the knee that persuade John he ought to comply with my repeated commands to get down on the ground.

After what has felt like for ever, my team finally arrive and help me to detain him. I manage to get the handcuffs on. I manage to tell him he's nicked. And, as the adrenalin subsides, I sink back onto the ground. John is carted off and an ambulance arrives. I tell them I've got a headache and that my neck is feeling sore. They respond by strapping me onto a body board and taping me into a head-and-neck brace. I suspect that I look ridiculous.

Off to Chelsea and Westminster Hospital, where I sit and wait to be seen. I send a couple of the team to knock on Bear's front door. I don't want to alarm her, but I do want her to be with me. I'm not looking my best, but she arrives and takes it in her stride. Over the next twenty-four hours, my face swells up nicely. My top lip looks as though it's been stung by the whole hive. I'm off work for the rest of the week.

I find out later that the milkman was, in fact, an off-duty Kiwi police officer. You couldn't make it up. He was travelling the world and earning some pocket money along the way. I never did get to thank him, but I'm so very glad he was there.

John gets six months. I get stitches in my mouth and a card from my boss with a picture of a duck on the front of it. To remind me what to do the next time someone throws a punch.

*

The assault has more of an effect on me than I am comfortable to admit. For a long period afterwards, I feel nervous out on the street. It's a new sensation for someone who has always jumped into whatever challenge might present itself but, even out on patrol with a colleague, I'm hesitant when dealing with strangers and with the unknown.

I don't tell anyone though. That wouldn't do. I'm the boss. I'm a bloke. Suck it up and get on with it. So I attempt to carry on regardless and wait for the feelings to pass. Eventually, they will and the unspoken memories and emotions will be buried away with a thousand others.

*

At the start of 2002, I head off on a skiing holiday with a bunch of friends. Bear has stayed back in London and I'm sitting alone on a chair lift when I decide that I'm going to do it. I'm going ask her to marry me. As I return home, I'm absolutely terrified. It will be the bravest thing I ever do in my life. Not because I have any doubts about her, but because I have endless doubts about me. She says yes and she changes my life. Fear has always been a bad reason not to do a good thing.

It's the catalyst to get back in touch with Dad. We've drifted apart in a sea of memories and sadness and I haven't spoken to him for the best part of two years. I never stopped loving him. It's just that loving him hurt too much and distance was easier. But this is news I need to tell him. I take Bear down to meet him and father and son begin again.

We get married in June of that year and Dad is a guest at the wedding. It will be the first time in about fifteen years that the Sutherlands – Mum, Dad, my sisters and me – have been in the same place at the same time and I'm more nervous about that than I am about anything else.

Familial anxieties apart, two memories of the day will stand out more than any other. First the vows – when the rest of the congregation fade and it is just Bear and me, making our promises, exchanging our rings, beginning our adventure, within the love of God. And then comes the reception and the arrival on stage of the house band, made up of old friends and former Fat & Frantic members. A couple of numbers in, they invite me to take the microphone and I lead them through a half-decent rendition of 'I Saw Her Standing There'.

I'm singing to my bride. She is my family now and this is just the start.

VII. *Management*

Having set out on married life, I find out that I've managed to negotiate my way through another promotion process. I apply for, and get, the job of Chief Inspector (Operations) at Croydon in south London. I will be responsible for the emergency response teams and for policing football matches at Crystal Palace.

And I'm a matter of weeks away from taking up the new post when I get a call from my current Borough Commander at Hammersmith. 'You're not going to Croydon,' she says.

'I'm not?'

'No.'

'But I've been for an interview and everything. The superintendent there told me I'd got the job.'

'I know.'

'So what's happening?'

'You're going to work for the Commissioner in his private office.'

'Blimey...'

I'm very reluctant to give up the prospect of an operational job, but the simple fact is that you don't say no to the Commissioner. I've met Sir John Stevens a couple of times, but I'm one of thousands – tens of thousands in fact. Still, for reasons that will never be explained to me, he's decided that he wants me in his office, writing speeches and picking up whatever else might come my way.

He's a remarkable man: tall in stature, large in personality and capable of inspiring and terrifying in equal measure. He's the only man I've ever met about whom practically every story you've ever heard is true. He's a bit of a legend. With a bit of a temper.

He's good enough to give me responsibilities in addition to the wordsmithing and I'm given the opportunity to accompany him on a number of trips and visits. Wherever we go, he is the star of the show: the keynote speaker, the guest of honour, the reviewing officer, the one with all the medals and the braid. But, without fail, he's always got time for the PC on the door. He always stops to talk to them. A proper conversation and a thank you. It's a couple of minutes for him, but it means the world to them as they grow an inch or two in the shadow of his uniform. These things matter.

*

The Commissioner is getting ready to launch a new neighbourhood policing programme alongside the Prime Minister and the Mayor of London. It's a big deal, given the rank and status of those involved. I get involved with all sorts of planning meetings with people from Number 10 and, at the end of one of them, I'm invited to listen in on the Prime Minister's press briefing.

Tony Blair has recently started holding a regular presidential-style Q&A with the media and I'm offered a place at the back of the room. With security tight, the journalists have to surrender their phones on the way in. But, as a trusted officer of the law, I'm allowed to keep mine. So I shuffle in and take my seat. Sir John is a demanding boss and I haven't dared switch my phone off in case he calls. But I am sure I've switched it to silent. I'm an idiot.

The PM is in full flow as the Nokia tune sounds boldly and loudly in my pocket. I make a frantic grab and press every button in rapid and repeated succession, but the sodding thing just keeps ringing. The nation's elected leader gives me a withering glance and I am surrounded by punishing glares and silent tutting. It is absolutely excruciating. Somehow, though, I make it out of Downing Street without being thrown in the Tower.

*

The Boss has a habit of appearing unannounced at our office door, located just down the corridor from his own. One afternoon, towards the end of normal office hours, I'm sitting quietly opposite Colette, his Staff Officer, when he appears at our door and orders us to follow. I'm out of my seat and after him straight away. I know by now that it's never a good idea to keep him waiting. And I'm intrigued to find out what he might want.

Turns out he simply wants to set the world to rights – over a glass of rather fine champagne. His door clicks shut behind the three of us and he produces the bottle. I sit there, wide-eyed and compliant, speaking when spoken to and sipping from my glass. I'm certain this wasn't in the job description.

*

Back at the flat, Bear emerges from the bathroom with the little plastic stick in her hand. 'I'm pregnant,' she says, grinning.

As I fold her in my arms and take in the wonder of it all, I feel a whispered sense of apprehension. Am I ready to be a dad? I still don't know if I'm ready to be a man. But at twelve weeks we head to the hospital for the scan and I see for the first time the miracle of new life – the insistent pulse of light on the screen that is our baby's heartbeat.

We will call her Jessie, and when I stare into her blue eyes, I will rediscover what it is to fall in love.

*

Family joy and sorrow intermingle. Mum's health has taken another turn for the worse. She has been diagnosed with a degenerative liver condition and has been told that she'll need a transplant. She has a rare blood type and so goes straight to the top of the waiting list. With that news comes the realisation that Mum's life is going to depend on someone else's death. Her condition continues to deteriorate, to the point that she needs permanent help at home. And Dad volunteers.

A little while earlier, he had moved to a monastery much closer to her and, quietly, she had settled into a routine of dropping by once a week for a cuppa and a conversation.

They had so much in common, and perhaps old wounds had started to heal a little.

So Dad moves into the spare room at Mum's. He cooks, he cleans, he washes, he mows. He takes care of her. And he will remain with her for the rest of his life. He turns half her garden shed into a little chapel and that's where he says his prayers. Time passes. Mum gets her transplant. Dad finds fragments of peace.

※

Meanwhile, the Commissioner is approaching retirement and I'm in the market for a new posting. The Borough Commander at Hammersmith gives me a call and invites me back. I'm immediately delighted by the prospect. Twelve months in an office have been more than enough – and the wonderful responsibilities that go with being a dad haven't dimmed my desire to get back to the frontline.

My new office is in the old Shepherd's Bush nick, a monstrous carbuncle just down from the Green on the Uxbridge Road. I'm given responsibility for the borough's neighbourhood policing teams and for building up our joint-working capabilities with the community safety and youth services run by the local authority.

※

In the summer of 2006, I become a dad for the second time. Daughter number two is Charlie and I fall head over heels all over again. But what kind of world will she be growing up in?

※

It's early 2007 and London finds itself in the midst of a grim succession of teenage murders.

On New Year's Day, Stephen Boachie is stabbed in east London. He was seventeen years old.

On 9 January, Dean Lahlou is stabbed in north London. He was eighteen years old.

On 3 February, James Smartt-Ford is shot in south London. He was sixteen.

On 6 February, Michael Dosunmu is shot in his own home in south London. He was fifteen.

On 14 February, Billy Cox is shot in south London. He was fifteen.

And so it continues. By the end of the year, twenty-six teenagers will have lost their lives on London's streets. But for the extraordinary advances in trauma care and the life-saving skills of police officers, paramedics and A&E staff, I don't doubt that the number would be significantly higher.

Twenty-six lives. Twenty-six families. Twenty-six sets of friends. Twenty-six neighbourhoods and communities. Twenty-six groups of suspects and their families too. All shattered.

The rest of the world will notice for a while – and then move on, attention taken by the next helping of celebrity gossip.

*

On 14 March 2007, Kodjo Yenga is murdered. The crime has happened on my patch – in Hammersmith Grove, West London – during the early evening of what is otherwise an entirely unremarkable weekday. I'm on a District Line train when my phone rings with the news. In the hours that follow, the facts begin to emerge. Kodjo was an A-Level student who had never been in contact, much less trouble, with the police. He was hunted down in the street by a pack of young suspects. And knifed to death.

Flowers begin to appear in the place where he fell. Friends, fellow teenagers, leave grief graffiti on the wall at the side of the road.

One afternoon a few days after his murder, I find myself standing in full uniform in the middle of Hammersmith Grove. It's a broad residential street a few hundred yards from the endless flow of Hammersmith Broadway and we've stopped the local traffic to allow Kodjo's family and friends to visit the scene.

Standing at a respectful distance, I watch as they gather. And I listen as wailing intertwines with the singing of hymns. It is magnificent and mournful and hopeful and hopeless. He was only sixteen, and he died in his girlfriend's arms.

*

The Murder Investigation Team (MIT), supported by local officers, do an exceptional job. They identify eyewitnesses and take lengthy statements from them: permanent records of the agonising accounts of those who were there when it happened. They carry out house-to-house enquiries. Where were local people when it happened? Did they see anything? Did they hear anything? Can they offer any scrap of information that might help?

Then there are the forensics, the phone records and the contents of dozens of past intelligence reports. Investigators trawl through CCTV footage and compile a sequence of images that show much of what happened on that March afternoon. They find Kodjo in the shopping centre at Hammersmith Broadway at about 4.30 p.m. He's there with Cookie, his girlfriend. And it's there that he meets with and speaks to one of the boys who challenges him to a fight and who will become a murderer before the day is out. The reasons for the challenge are unclear. Some young people will talk about respect and status and the desire for certain boys to prove themselves as big men. But it is impossible to make any real sense of what follows.

Recordings from successive cameras track Kodjo and Cookie away from the Broadway and into Hammersmith Grove. They also reveal the movements of a growing group of suspects. The final, fatal, cowardly and catastrophic acts take place out of shot.

Within days, the team have made a number of arrests. Almost all of them are children and some of them are as young as eleven years old. I find myself asking how on earth it came to this. I sit down with colleagues from the local authority and we determine to look into the backgrounds, the stories, of all those suspected of any kind of involvement in this act of unfathomable madness. The idea is to identify any common threads – any possible reasons to explain how these things come to pass.

We take our time. When the results come through they are, on the one hand, startling and, on the other, not surprising at all. There are some consistent elements in the backgrounds of many of the young people we're concerned about. Most come from broken homes, many have been excluded from education at some point in their young lives, some (though by no means all) have previous criminal histories and some have older siblings who are involved in crime.

But one fact stands out clear from all the others. Every single one of them has grown up in a home where domestic violence has been a reality. Not a single exception. Now try telling me there's no link.

*

The local authority arrange a workshop with a large group of young people, all similar ages to Kodjo and his killers, all living in similar neighbourhoods and attending similar schools. Among any number of important issues for debate, there is one particularly critical question that we want to ask them: what can we, as adults, do to help you, as young people, feel safer? And, among a range of thoughtful and intelligent answers, all unprompted, the one that stands out to me most clearly is this: 'We want the police to do more Stop & Search.'

It catches me by surprise. I had grown used to the suggestion that Stop & Search was a power that caused resentment, particularly among teenagers. But, with this group at least, I was wrong. You see, young people know far better than the rest of us just how many knives and other weapons are being carried out there. Most understand with particular clarity and immediacy the lethal threat posed by the knife carriers and they recognise the critical need for the violent to be challenged. They absolutely want us to use the power but – and this is every bit as important – they want us to use it professionally and well.

*

The conversations continue in the weeks following Kodjo's death. I find myself walking along the street, deep in an exchange with a senior member of staff from the Westminster Youth Offending Service. There's a YOS in every London borough and the staff there work with young people who end up in the Criminal Justice System, suspected of all manner of criminality.

My colleague starts speaking about one teenage boy who is giving her team particular cause for concern. 'The thing is,' she says to me, 'we don't think he knows what dying is.' I look at her with what is, I suspect, a puzzled expression on my face. She goes on to say that this boy has played so many violent video games in which he is killed, only to get up and carry on shooting, that he genuinely has no concept of the finality of death. My bemusement turns to disbelief, until I see it for what it is.

He has no other frame of reference, no understanding of true consequences, no comprehension of the fact that if he were to carry a knife – even for his own protection – the person most likely to be stabbed with it is him. And he has no insight into the fact that joining a street gang is likely to make him less safe, not more. No appreciation of the fact that real life just isn't like a video game.

*

The journalist Andrew Anthony tells the full story of Kodjo Yenga's murder in an *Observer* article headlined 'The Killing of Kodjo'. As I was one of the officers involved in the local response to the case, he asked to interview me as part of his research for the piece – and our conversations about the life and death of an innocent young man will stay with me for the rest of my days.

Andrew asks me why the violence is happening and whether I think things are getting worse. I tell him that things are certainly changing: that those involved are getting younger, that the level of violence used is growing, that the speed at which incidents escalate is accelerating. Technology plays a part. During my school days in the seventies and early eighties, a potentially provocative rumour would take all day to circulate and, likely as not, would have run out of steam by the time we were all kicked out at the end of lessons. Since the advent of social media, hours have become seconds and no one is afforded the opportunity to sift error from fact.

Andrew has an interest in the cultural context within which an inordinate number of youth killings are taking place. Among a number of other questions, he asks me whether I think the musician 50 Cent is to blame, pointing out that the violence and misogyny apparent in so much rap music has been a recurring theme in recent media commentary. In replying I suggest that while I don't think that 50 Cent (or anyone else for that matter) is directly responsible, I do have a strong view about a combination of influences that I consider to be enormously damaging.

These influences in themselves are not what makes a person vulnerable but, without any doubt, they prey upon and exacerbate the vulnerabilities already present in so many damaged lives.

Taken together, the deeply harmful content available to young people through the internet, through films, through music and through video games, alongside the dulling, desensitising effects of real-life atrocities repeated on twenty-four-hour news loops, has the potential to do untold harm to those who are exposed to it. Frankly, anyone attempting to brush off the risks associated with allowing anyone – never mind those who are particularly susceptible to harm – unrestricted access to hardcore and extreme content is being wilfully stupid.

I'm not just a police officer. I'm a Londoner, a husband and a dad. And these are our children.

*

Kodjo's case will eventually get to court more than a year after the killing and two boys, by then aged seventeen and fourteen, will be convicted of murder. Three other boys, aged fourteen, fifteen and seventeen at the time of the trial, will be convicted of manslaughter. His story ends there, but the memory of it will always stay with me.

*

I'm standing in the first-floor corridor at Hammersmith Police Station and I'm practically shouting into my mobile. As any of my colleagues will tell you, it's not my usual style. On the other end of the line is a local councillor and he knows I'm onto him. He's taken some police data I've provided, deliberately manipulated and misrepresented it and then, without saying anything to me in advance, published it in a crass attempt to gain some sort of marginal advantage over his political opponents. I'm not quite sure what he calls it, but I call it lying. He makes a cack-handed effort to defend his position, but he's not even fooling himself.

End of phone call, end of almost any possibility of a constructive working relationship. Right now, there are people in the cells downstairs I would trust more than him.

The thing is, though, we're all capable of it: playing games with numbers, massaging figures to suit agendas, selling our souls along the way. And for what? It certainly isn't going to make anyone any safer.

*

Still at Hammersmith. Members of our Crime Squad have saved the life of a critically injured drug dealer. Responding to a call, they find him lying in the street, bleeding heavily. He has been stabbed through the femoral artery and is in a bad way. But he is a violent and dangerous man and, unbelievably, he wants to fight the officers who are trying to save his life. It's all he knows.

One of the PCs actually puts his foot into the man's groin in a desperate attempt to stop the bleeding. The dealer survives. And he never says thank you.

One of the great pleasures of leadership is to be found in the celebration of what people achieve. I'm so struck by the actions of the Crime Squad in this instance that I nominate them for a fast-track Commissioner's Commendation. My recommendation meets with approval and I find myself actually blinking back some unexpected tears as I call them into the office to tell them about the recognition that's coming their way.

*

Young people continue to be at the heart of my personal and professional concerns. This afternoon, I'm the Match Commander for a Premier League game at Craven Cottage, the home of Fulham Football Club. It's a friendly place to watch a game of football, with rarely a hint of crowd trouble.

The control room is a cramped box at the back of the Main Stand and I'm sitting, binoculars in hand, alongside the club's safety officer as the match gets underway. Midway through an uneventful first half, the PC monitoring the small bank of CCTV screens calls over to me. On one of them, he points out a group of youngsters up at the back of the Away Section – a girl and three or four boys who don't look much more than eighteen or so. And something about their behaviour just isn't right, not least the fact that they appear to have little or no interest in what's happening on the pitch.

The camera stays on them and, to our absolute astonishment, the girl ducks down and appears to start performing an oral sex act on one of the boys. In broad daylight. In front of tens of thousands of football fans. The footage isn't conclusive, but it doesn't leave much to the imagination. I'm horrified.

We send officers to investigate, my overwhelming concern being for the welfare of the girl. How old is she? Who is she with? Is she really doing what we think she's doing? Is she a willing participant in whatever is happening or is she acting under some form of duress?

The PCs find her in the crowd and take her somewhere discreet – away from the boys and away from the noise – to give her the time and space to say anything she wants or needs to say. And she says nothing, at least, nothing of any significance. There are no disclosures, no allegations of crime or any other form of unwarranted behaviour – and she is an adult, albeit a very young one. In the absence of any third-party report or clear evidence of an offence, there is nothing more we can do. But I am in state of disbelief. The relentless sexualisation of society is running away from us. And I fear that we will be left with the consequences for generations.

*

Late turn at Shepherd's Bush. One of the Special Constables based at the station is an old friend of mine. His name is Alex. For months, we've been telling one another that we really ought to head out on patrol together. Now Alex has accepted a job at the National Crime Agency and this evening is going to be the last opportunity we have before he hands his warrant card in.

We head out of the station and turn right towards the chatter and scurry of the shops on the Uxbridge Road. We've not gone far when a young lad races past us on the pavement. He doesn't break stride as we turn to look at him. Moments later, he's followed by a breathless and angry older man. 'He's stolen my phone...'

It's the sounding of the starter's pistol. I'm on my toes and putting it up on the radio simultaneously. 'Chasing robbery suspect... eastbound Uxbridge Road...'

He's younger than me, faster than me, fitter than me. And

he's not wearing boots, body armour and a full kit belt. The gap between us is growing, as he heads left off the main road. I shout a description down the radio and give an update on his direction of travel. He's still just about in sight. Alex paused to check that the victim was OK, before taking off after me. I keep running.

There's nothing quite like a good foot chase – though the ones you lose are significantly less enjoyable than the ones you win.

He rounds a corner up ahead of me and I get there just in time to see him disappear over the top of a six-foot-high wooden fence and into the first of a long row of terraced back gardens. I take a running jump at the fence and haul myself onto the top of it. My suspect has already vanished from view. As I take a moment to consider what to do next – and to listen for any noise that might give away his location or direction – I lose grip and balance. My mind slows down, but my body doesn't, covering the two-metre drop to the concrete on the other side in half a blink. I land heavily on my right-hand side and I feel like a fool, comforted only by the realisation that there are no witnesses to my unintended pratfall. I stand up slowly and reach for my ribs. Damn, they hurt.

By now, the helicopter's up, the Crime Squad are descending on the surrounding streets and the dog van is on the way. Somehow though, the suspect gets away and I have precisely nothing to show for my misadventures, except my injuries.

At home later on, I sit on the edge of the bed and lower myself back slowly onto the pillow, wincing with every breath. I blame Alex.

*

Back at Hammersmith, local officers are hosting a very special visitor. He's a former colleague, celebrating thirty years of retirement, after thirty years in the job. He must be approaching eighty years of age. Back in the day, he had been the driver of Foxtrot 1-1, the unmarked crime car based at Shepherd's Bush. And, after tea and buns, the team take him out for a spin in the modern equivalent. Then, without telling a soul, somewhere in the quiet backstreets near Wormwood Scrubs, they sit him back behind the wheel for one last blue-light run. Just for old times' sake.

VIII. *Hostage Negotiator*

For a number of years now, I've wanted to be a hostage negotiator. There might be any number of reasons why, but it certainly has something to do with caring about people – about what happens to them. And I would also have to confess to being drawn by the mystique and sense of adventure associated with the role.

I get through the selection process and find myself back at Hendon for the two-week residential course. It's relentlessly demanding, a succession of sixteen-hour days testing us to our limits and by far the best training I have ever taken part in. Passing the course is one of my proudest moments; deploying operationally will be one of my greatest privileges. In time, it will also take its toll.

*

I take my place on the negotiator on-call rota. Aside from the very small permanent team based at the Yard, the role is in addition to the day job. For seven days and nights, the phone is switched on constantly and the packed rucksack, filled with extra layers of clothing and assorted bits of kit, is never too far away. The call can come at any moment. Or not at all. Standing by.

If I'm at work when the phone rings, the expectation is that I will respond immediately – whatever I happen to be doing at the time can wait till later. If I'm at home, I will just drop everything and go.

The task is, in so many ways, a simple one. Phil – a friend and colleague who is a senior negotiator – will only ever ask one question when he rings to call you out: 'Are you ready to save a life?' And that's it. That's what it comes down to. Among all the inevitable complexity of broken lives, it's as straightforward and as profound as that. Saving lives.

Negotiators are optimists. You have to be, to see light in the darkest of situations and love in the most troubling of circumstances. But it's not an idle hope, it's an optimism born of years of experience. Almost every story will end well. Almost.

*

The first few calls come in the middle of the night. The phone rings insistently beside the bed and I reach for it as swiftly as the clutches of deep sleep will allow. I don't want to wake Bear and the girls if I can possibly help it, so I ask my nocturnal caller to hold the line while I hurry downstairs and flick the kitchen light on. I grab a piece of paper and start to take down whatever scant details are available. Often, it's just a location and a brief description of the circumstances: a man on a roof, a man on a crane, a man armed with a knife, a woman on a window ledge.

People in crisis. People in pieces. People on the edge. Men more often than women in my experience.

Sometimes I get cancelled before I manage to get out of the house. The first time I actually get to the scene, I play the role of silent partner as my more experienced colleague leads the way. It's over quickly and it ends well. It will be my turn soon enough.

It's extraordinary how alone people can feel in one of the largest and most vibrant cities on the planet. I've been called out to a sheltered housing block somewhere out in the wilds of east London. Now I'm sitting in a comfortable armchair in the communal lounge and seated opposite me is one of the elderly residents of the place. He's holding a knife.

Actually, he's threatening to cut his own throat with it and my job is to try everything to persuade him not to. Assorted police colleagues watch and listen in. Everything about the scene is incongruous, not least our being in a room more used to the murmur of quiet conversation and the clink of cup on saucer, where the elderly sit with blanketed knees and wait in the hope that the grandchildren might visit.

With staff and residents ushered to safety, the old man tells us his story and shares his despair. Late on in life, he's fallen in love with someone – a fellow inhabitant of the block. But she's having none of it and, by all accounts, has been pretty unpleasant to him along the way. This poor old boy is desperate and, it would appear, desperately lonely. I don't know whether he has any family and, if he does, where they are. At this particular moment in time, it looks and sounds as though it's just him.

Each negotiation is as different as the person you're faced with. What works with one may not work with another. It may, in fact, have precisely the opposite effect. I feel my way gently, listening intently to everything he says. Just as importantly, I listen to what he's not saying. I look for clues, for scraps, for anything I can latch onto and work with. I try to reason with him, to empathise with him, to offer comfort and encouragement.

I know you're having a bad day, but things can change. I know you're hurting, but it won't always feel like this. Let's talk about all the things you have to live for. My name is John, I'm with the police and I'm here to help you.

For a while, none of it seems to make any difference and the knife stays in place. None of us feels threatened by him. All of us are faster and stronger than he is. But that doesn't lessen the danger he presents to himself. There is no safe way of taking the knife from him, not without the risk of causing him serious injury. The only realistic option is to persuade him to put it down voluntarily. I try a different approach and, after a good deal of talk, he eventually agrees to do just that. The suggestion that he shouldn't give this woman who has rejected him the satisfaction of seeing him seriously hurt is the one that seems finally to get through. But the scene remains among the saddest I've ever seen. It is perhaps one of society's greatest failings that so many old people feel alone.

*

On a different afternoon, I find myself on the ground floor of a south London town hall. I'm sitting in one of those meeting booths – the ones where client and official are separated by Plexiglas. It's a bit like you might imagine a prison visiting facility to be, except with carpets. And the smell of air freshener.

But I'm not a customer. I've been called out from home. The man on the other side of the screen is unkempt, unshaven and dressed in scruffs. He's got heavily ringed eyes, weeks of dirt underneath his fingernails and a disconcerting collection of scabs and scars all over him. It's difficult to tell his age, but every line on his face seems to have been carved by sadness. He's holding a used hypodermic in his right hand and he's pressing it into an ugly, seeping wound in the side of his neck. He's threatening to inject air into his vein, to say nothing of the damage the needle itself might do.

He is a picture of endless despair. A man who has fallen out of the bottom of life. And so I talk to him. I listen to his story and I try to understand. It has something to do with a letter he's had from the Housing people and the possibility of eviction. He's evidently desperate. He rants and he rambles as I watch the needle wobble in and out of the hole in his neck. Steady now.

It's far from straightforward, but we get there in the end. He puts down the syringe and gives himself up. Local officers walk him away and that is the last I ever see of him. I've done what I was called out to do. I step back from his raw pain and return home to my family, wrenched from one world into another.

*

Romford, east London. Male armed with a knife threatening self-harm. Negotiators requested. I'm sitting at home none the wiser when my phone buzzes. On the other end of the line is one of my colleagues asking if I'm available to attend the call.

The number for the chief inspector in the main Met control room is saved in my mobile. I ring straight through with the call reference number and ask for a Fast Car run to the scene. A Traffic Unit is assigned.

I grab my rucksack and head to the end of my road – always my pick-up point of choice. Best not to have the blues and twos going outside the front door. I hear the sirens before I see the car. Then flat out. You never quite lose the simple thrill of it all. At least, I haven't.

The driver explains that Romford is too far off his patch, so he's called ahead and arranged for a second car to meet us at Tower Bridge. As we cross from south to north, they're waiting by the nearside kerb, a stone's throw from Tower Hill DLR station. The lights on the roof of their car are already going. I jump out of one BMW and start running towards the other. I bundle myself into the back and we're off again. I make my introductions and thank the two PCs for the ride.

At this point, as we pick up speed, I pause and say two silent prayers. One for the man with the knife and one that I don't throw up all over the back of the car. It's a long run on mostly straight roads and I pull my thoughts together, rehearsing possible opening lines in my head. I get occasional updates on the phone: he's holding a knife and local officers are trying to talk to him. It's suggested that he's suffering from an unspecified mental illness. The TSG have been assigned and are on the way. How's this one going to go? How does this particular story end?

Romford is miles away, but eventually we get there. My negotiating partner – travelling from a completely different point of the compass – has come across a serious crime en route and has had to make an arrest. He'll get to me eventually, but for now, I'm the only one here. And I'm supposed to be the expert.

I find the Duty Officer. What do we know? What's the plan? Contain and negotiate. Invariably the best option.

The drama is unfolding on one of those nondescript, new-build estates – a small cluster of characterless low-rise blocks built on cheap land close to the railway lines. My man is in the living room of a first-floor flat, holding a large knife to his own throat. I make my way up the communal stairs, past a line of uniforms. Everyone is here for the same, straight-forward reason: to get him out without anyone getting hurt.

I walk through the front door of the flat and step into the room. Immediately in front of me, there's a diagonal line of TSG officers, in full kit with long shields, partitioning the scene. Me on one side of them, him on the other. There's a strange sense of unreality to it all. I don't know this part of London. I don't know any of the other officers who are here. I don't know the young man facing me and I don't know his sorrows. I don't know what might happen next. So I start talking.

Within a very short space of time, a simple fact becomes

clear to me. Mine isn't the only voice he's hearing. I'm no medical expert of course, but years of frontline policing experience teach you to recognise the signs. None of my colleagues is making a sound, but he's only answering me intermittently. His eyes have a faraway look and, at times, he seems to be reacting to things I can neither see nor hear, prompts from somewhere inside his own head. I can only feel a deep sense of compassion. It's a hell of a way to be. He is pacing continually backwards and forwards in front of me – like the tiger I once saw in London Zoo – and the knife keeps returning to his throat.

'Care in the Community' they once called it. The ideal was that significant numbers of people suffering from mental illness should be cared for within the communities where they live. Whatever it was meant to achieve, it isn't working. Not for this poor man. And not in so many places where I've worked. That's not to decry the efforts of any number of extraordinarily dedicated and caring mental-health profes-sionals. It's simply that demand is greater than supply. And by some distance.

Backwards and forwards he walks. He hasn't put the knife down, but at least he hasn't drawn blood. Time passes. I wouldn't be surprised if the TSG officers were cramping up a bit. They've been standing in the same position, in heavy kit, for a good while now. Other negotiators arrive and we take our turns. Normally, the preference would be to keep going for as long as possible, building a rapport and the beginnings of a relationship. But not with this troubled soul. We change over every few minutes, simply to vary the voices in the hope that one or other of us might just get through. None of it seems to work. One minute he's with us and partly lucid, the next minute he's somewhere else entirely.

Eventually, though, we get a breakthrough. His mum is on the phone and, after some discussion, the consensus among the negotiators is that it will do more good than harm for her to speak to him. But we know it's still a risk. What if she triggers something in him? What if she has played some contributory part in his descent into serious illness? But what if he refuses to put the knife down? What if he uses it to hurt himself? Or one of us? Nothing is simple or straightforward in the places where police officers find themselves.

His mum comes through for us. And for him. She's the one who persuades him to put the knife down and to surrender. All of our experience added up to not a great deal, but it ended OK. And no one got hurt. We get to go home, perhaps with a small amount of professional satisfaction, more though in the knowledge that there's so much in life to be thankful for. But what about him? And so many others like him? He doesn't need to be handcuffed in the back of a police van, he needs expert medical care. He doesn't need to be in a police cell, he needs to be in hospital.

*

And there are so many other stories I could tell you: the man with a meat cleaver in the communal hallway of a block of flats; the overdosed woman, teetering on the edge of a first-floor roof, lapsing into unconsciousness; the man standing beside an icy pond in the pitch darkness, threatening to jump; the man who has smashed his way up and out of the loft space at the top of a terraced house, covering himself in blue paint in the process and now hurling roof tiles onto the street below; the man who has barricaded himself into a flat, holding a baby in his right arm as he gesticulates wildly with his left. And then there are those we don't get to in time. We do what we can.

IX. *The Shadows of Terror*

On 9/11, I was away on holiday in South Wales with Bear and her family: watching airliners fall, half a world away. Our own reckoning was coming.

*

I am on duty on 7/7, but in a part of London not directly affected. In fact, I'm talking to a colleague in his office at Brixton Police Station when news begins to filter through of a possible power surge on the Underground system. We all know what became of those first reports, and so begins my flat-out dash to my own station in west London. With no hope of public transport, I run home. I grab my pushbike and get to Fulham as fast as I can. This great city isn't just my place of work. It's my home, it's where my family lives, it's where my children are growing up, and we are under attack.

The rest of the day is a blur of briefings, deployments, questions without answers and the sense of being in the middle of the unknown.

The death toll rises.

That evening, I join the rest of the country in front of the television, trying to make some kind of sense of it all. Yesterday we celebrated the hosting of the Olympic Games being awarded to London. Today, 7 July 2005, everything is different.

*

The following morning, at around 6 a.m., I make my way into the briefing room at Shepherd's Bush, where I join the officers parading for the early shift. There's none of the usual larking or joking. No banter. There's a different kind of atmosphere: sober, silent, still. And I hear myself talking to the group of PCs in front of me about suicide bombers. Not as some abstract reality in another part of the world, but as a clear and present danger in the neighbourhoods we serve. I can hear myself telling them to be careful out there. And meaning it like I've never meant it before. It just feels unreal.

*

In the days immediately following the bombings, we deploy officers to fixed points at every Tube station in London. The weather is startlingly hot and the PCs are wearing full kit and body armour, topped off with high-visibility, non-breathable jackets. The effects of this particular sartorial combination are not dissimilar to wearing a bin bag while doing sit-ups in a sauna.

I'm on my way to a meeting and I stop to talk to the two officers standing outside Parsons Green station. They're in good spirits. No one is complaining because everyone knows what's at stake. But they are melting.

As I leave them behind, I'm approached by a passer-by – a

local Fulham resident. In a voice even posher than my own, he says, 'Excuse me, would you mind if I bought your officers an ice cream?' I smile. Of course I wouldn't. It's the very least they deserve. And, for a while, London appreciates its police officers and other emergency services workers as never before.

*

Several years later, I will take up my post as Borough Commander of Camden. I arrive there just at the time the 7/7 inquests are being held. Camden, arguably, feels it more than any other borough. Three of the four devices were detonated there and a number of my new colleagues wear the insignia of a Commissioner's High Commendation on their uniforms. Awarded in only the most exceptional of circumstances, it serves as a permanent reminder of the courage and humanity they showed on that fateful July day.

Having had the experience of giving evidence at a high-profile inquest, I offer to support one local officer who has been called to take the stand. Before I speak to him, I read his statement. It is simple and straightforward, without embellishment or obvious emotion. Just the facts, as the saying goes. But it is shattering.

After the Underground had been hit, amid the chaos and confusion, officers were despatched to multiple locations in and around King's Cross. This particular PC found himself in Tavistock Square. He was there when the bus exploded. He saw it happen. In his statement, he describes the noise and what begins to unfold in front of him. He acts on instinct and begins to walk towards the shattered double-decker. As everybody scatters in absolute panic, he breaks into a jog and then a sprint. He is running flat out towards the very thing that practically everybody else is trying desperately to get away from. He steps onto the bus and into a kind of waking hell. He sees things that defy description and is forced to make decisions – who to help, who is beyond help – that are impossible to grasp fully. Those of us who weren't there will never truly know. But I salute him and every other member of the emergency services and every member of the public who displayed the very best of humanity that day. In the face of the very worst.

*

Nine years after the bombings, I'm sitting outside a pub in west London one afternoon in early summer. Opposite me is one of the survivors of 7/7. He was on the Tube at Edgware Road that July day. He was sitting a matter of feet away from the bomber, rehearsing lines for a Shakespeare production he was due to appear in and, by rights, he ought not to have survived. But he did and I'm both humbled and honoured to spend a bit of time in the company of this extraordinary man. He's missing one of his legs as well as his pancreas and he struggles with the hearing in one ear. His life was saved by a combination of fellow passengers, a paramedic and a Met officer who went down into the tunnels. He keeps in touch with all of them, and he remains deeply grateful.

One phrase he uses, among many others, impresses me particularly deeply. He says, 'Most people seem to think that 7/7 was all about hate. My own experience was one of love.' The love of friends and strangers. The love of police officers and paramedics, of firefighters and Underground staff. The love of fellow survivors.

Then, as he sits across the table from me, he pats his artificial leg and, all of a sudden, quotes from *Henry V*:

He that shall live this day, and see old age,
Will yearly on the vigil feast his neighbours,
And say 'To-morrow is Saint Crispian:'
Then will he strip his sleeve and show his scars.
And say 'These wounds I had on Crispin's day.'
Old men forget: yet all shall be forgot,
But he'll remember with advantages
What feats he did that day…

Remarkable, remarkable man.

Then there's the PC who helped to save his life. Dave was part of a three-man armed patrol unit with a pan-London role on the morning of 7/7. The calls were beginning to come thick and fast, still with no clarity about what on earth was happening. They were not far from Edgware Road. They called up on the radio and offered to attend. They were instructed to continue with their armed duties instead. But something told them that they should go all the same. They all felt it.

They arrived at the Tube station and saw a deserted ambulance, back doors wide open, parked in the middle of the road, followed by dozens of members of the public, stumbling out of the station entrance, filthy and bleeding. While his two colleagues began immediate first aid with the people in front of them, Dave went in. He descended to the platform. He entered the tunnel. He went down into the darkness. He hadn't gone far before he came across an obviously dead body. He went deeper in and found the carriage where the bomb had exploded. And, like his colleague in Tavistock Square, he saw things that are beyond imagining for most of us.

Among all the carnage, he could hear someone moaning – one passenger who was still alive, among the bodies of those who were not so fortunate. It was the man who later sat opposite me at the pub. Dave went no further. Here was a life to be saved. He improvised bandages from torn strips of clothing and, together with others, did what he could until further help arrived.

When later asked at the inquest why he had gone down into the tunnels that day, he replied simply, 'Because I was there'. I can only hope I would have done the same. I doubt you'd recognise his full name and his story won't have been told in too many places. But he is a true hero. He isn't the only one.

*

On 21 July 2005, London is attacked again. Four more bombs on the public transport system, but this time they fail to go off. One of the devices is at Shepherd's Bush Green Underground station. A discarded rucksack, abandoned on the platform, is giving off intermittent puffs of smoke. The suspect was last seen running north on the rail tracks. It's all a matter of 400 yards from my office window.

I'm at a meeting with a local community leader on the

other side of the Green and I'm not even in uniform. The phone rings with the news, I offer my hurried apologies and start running to the scene. The control van is setting up nearby. I grab a yellow reflective jacket and stand by. Reports are coming through of other, similarly unexploded, devices elsewhere in London.

I don't do anything brave or brilliant as the day wears on. It falls to me to marshal the overwhelming numbers of journalists and camera people who are descending on the scene. We hold them behind a makeshift cordon. They are desperate to know what the hell is going on. So am I. I try to ring Bear to let her know I'm fine and manage to get through.

The following day, back in uniform, I'm outside the Tube station talking to a DS from the Anti-Terrorist Branch. The scene is still locked down and a massive manhunt is underway. His phone rings. He ends the call, looks at me and tells me that we've shot the wrong man. At Stockwell.

I feel a physical sensation not far from pain somewhere in my gut. It's a situation too dreadful to contemplate. For everyone. The terrorists failed yesterday, but today another innocent life has been lost.

X. *Up North London*

Another year, another change of rank and role. Adrian, my old friend from Fulham days, is now a DCI in north London and he gives his Borough Commander a nudge. Within a few weeks, I discover that I'm going to be the superintendent in charge of uniform policing in Islington. It's an extraordinary opportunity. Islington is a busy patch of London and I will have the task of leading the hundreds of officers and support staff responsible for emergency response and neighbourhood policing in the borough.

*

In my last couple of weeks in west London, I had been battling a severe chest infection and I take it with me to my new post. It's terrible timing. The symptoms worsen, but I'm determined to make a positive start in the new job. So I start early and I work long hours. I visit my teams and go out on patrol with them, because first impressions matter. But, beneath my body armour, I'm drenched with sweat and running a high temperature.

I keep going for a fortnight but, with no improvement in sight, I go very reluctantly to see my GP. She examines me and then looks at me with a serious expression on her face. She tells me that I am showing all the signs of the early stages of pneumonia. She tells me that if I don't stop and take a break straight away, I am going to make myself very seriously ill.

I had been hospitalised with pneumonia as a teenager and I know how bad it can be. I am persuaded of the need to rest. I go home to bed and I barely move for a week. Even then, I probably go back to work too quickly. I suppose my own health seems a relatively minor consideration, given all the agonies that this line of work reveals.

There's something about policing that makes it so hard to set aside: the just and noble cause, the undeniable and aching need in homes and neighbourhoods, the calls that keep on coming, the sense of adventure, the desire to go on making a difference. I suspect that I'm so preoccupied with looking after everyone else, that I neglect to look after myself as I should. This job can take it out of you.

*

It's a Sunday afternoon in June 2008 and I'm at home in the kitchen, doing plenty of not much at all. Bear and the children are upstairs. The radio is on in the background – BBC 5 Live – and I pause at the sink to listen to the headlines. Yet another teenager has been murdered in London. Another victim of knife crime; another wasted life; another shattered family; another hopeless statistic; another round of hand-wringing.

Except that this one is different. They all are, of course, but this one is different for me. Along with a small handful of others, it will become one of the stories that has the greatest impact of any in my policing life. It happened on my patch in Islington late last night. The victim was sixteen years old. His sister is a well-known actress and the media are giving it the full treatment. The diary might have this down as a day off, but that is of no consequence now.

I'm straight onto the phone, first to colleagues and then to partners in the local authority, piecing together the facts and coming up with a plan of action. The Murder Team will pick up the immediate investigation but the fallout will come to us.

His name was Ben Kinsella and I never had the honour of knowing him.

The following day continues to be dominated by the aftermath of the murder: meetings with the Senior Investigating Officer, with local community representatives and with my own officers. There are killers to catch, a family to comfort and a community to reassure.

On Tuesday, there's a press briefing scheduled with members of Ben's family, to be hosted by us at the station. The day arrives and our conference room is absolutely heaving. George and Brooke, Ben's dad and sister, arrive early and are shown to my office. For a few short minutes, it's just me and the two of them. They are grey and bewildered – undone by grief – and I am struggling to find the right thing to say. I tell them how deeply sorry I am. I tell George that no father should ever have to bury his son. And I make a stumbling promise to do everything in my power to make sure that no other family has to find themselves in this desperate place. I'm not sure any of it registers. And why should it? They are adrift in the face of their sorrow.

As they head down the corridor to face the cameras, I am left alone with my thoughts. First Kodjo; now Ben. There have been others, of course, but these are the two cases that I've had first-hand dealings with. Two innocents lost in horrendous circumstances. They might have been my brothers. They might have been my sons.

*

As the investigation into Ben's murder progresses, four possible suspects are identified. Two of them are siblings and their background grabs my attention. They are still only teenagers but, earlier in their young lives, they had witnessed their father's attempt to kill their mother. One of the brothers is later convicted of Ben's murder. The other brother wasn't involved, but has his own grim set of circumstances. And it's not difficult to make a connection. Because violence begets violence.

Of course, not every young person raised in a violent home will themselves grow up to become violent. The reality is much more hopeful than that. But my experience of those young men who do go on to cause serious harm is that it all began behind closed doors – hidden in their homes and their childhoods. It's one of the undeniable conclusions of my professional life.

*

The day of Ben's funeral arrives. The service will be taken by Father Jim, a wonderful local Catholic priest and a friend of the Kinsella family.

Dressed in my number-one uniform and accompanied by my boss, I walk the short distance to the church. The pavements outside are overflowing. Inside, it is standing room only. Along with the Senior Investigating Officer from the Murder Team, we are shown to reserved seats a couple of rows back, just behind the family. I feel a sense of guilt, partly that I am stepping into a grief that doesn't belong to me, partly some half-formed and unspoken thought that my colleagues and I could, should, have done more to prevent this ghastly nightmare from ever happening.

The service is beautiful and I am stirred deeply.

*

A couple of years later, I find myself on an industrial estate in north London, just round the corner from Finsbury Park Tube. I'm heading for a new exhibition curated by the Ben Kinsella Trust, founded by his family in his memory. I've got some colleagues with me from Camden's Gangs Team. I want them to hear Ben's story – this story that has left such a mark on me.

Brooke is there to meet us with her and Ben's mum, Debbie. I love these people – for their courage and their dignity, for their insistence that something good should come out of it all and for their friendship.

The exhibition is both a wonderful celebration of a re-markable young life and a captivating, heartbreaking lesson about the realities of knife crime. As we sit in darkness, watching silent black-and-white CCTV footage of Ben stumbling down the road moments after having been stabbed, I quietly weep.

One day, when I look back over the course of my policing life, I will remember standing at far too many murder scenes, in the haunted places where young men have lost their lives. Here in Islington, as the world's attention moves on, I am left with a sense of professional responsibility and determination beyond anything I've experienced before. I cannot stand by and let this madness continue to repeat itself. And, anyway, I made a promise to Ben's dad.

*

There have been other murders in north London and, perfectly understandably, there is enormous local community concern. I will never shy away from the duties that we have: to patrol the streets, to stop and to search, to challenge the violent, to be the first on scene, to be a source of comfort for a family, to lead the hunt for those responsible, to seek justice on behalf of those no longer able to seek it for themselves. But there is, too, a realisation that we aren't simply going to arrest our way out of this – that policing is, in fact, just one small part of the puzzle. Enforcement is a critical means of stemming the flow but, on its own, is no more than a patch-up job. Something more is required.

The first step for us is to set up a police Youth Engagement Team (YET) in the borough. It's one of the first of its kind in the country and I handpick five officers with a very specific skill. I choose them, primarily, for their ability to communicate. I want them out there engaging with young people – on the streets, in youth clubs and even in their homes. When a young person comes to our notice as being of concern, the YET will carry out a home visit, sitting down with teenager and parent (usually Mum), confronting their behaviour and explaining the potential consequences of the things they're involved in. They will look for appropriate diversion opportunities – education, sport, music, art, whatever – operating alongside trained youth workers in the process. Some might argue that we are straying beyond our core policing role, but I can't think of another way to begin changing the repetition of sorry experience.

The second step is to develop a multi-agency capability. Whatever we do needs to be a partnership undertaking – so we work with the Islington council's community safety and youth offending teams, with schools, with pupil referral units, with Arsenal Football Club's community team and with local youth clubs and charities. There is an absolute acknowledgement that no agency is likely to achieve anything of lasting significance by working in isolation. The reality is that knife crime and the senseless deaths of a procession of young men are a 'whole society' problem. One that demands a 'whole society' solution.

Step three is to change the way in which we go about some of our 'normal' policing business. When we have the TSG working in the borough for example, in vans with six or seven officers on board, tasked with specific enforcement work, we send one of the YET PCs with them as a spotter: with their local knowledge and communication skills, they are able to direct their colleagues to the right areas and to the right people.

Stop & Search needs to be used intelligently, not indiscriminately. And the nature of street encounter between young people and police officers really matters. Every contact leaves a trace.

When we have a violent incident involving young people (or even the threat of one), we deploy the YET and the council's youth workers into the affected neighbourhood, alongside the more conventional emergency response. The aim is to support any investigation and to prevent escalation or reprisals. Over time, it seems to do some good, because we start to see less youth violence.

But there is no sense of 'job done'. History will continue to repeat itself. I will find myself here again. I know that there is a need to go further still and to try to comprehend why the hell a young man would pick up and use a knife in the first place. I think of the boys who murdered Kodjo; I think of the boys who murdered Ben. And I try to imagine every person – overwhelmingly young men – caught up in serious violence. It strikes me that it is so much easier to judge someone than it is to try to understand them. We should never attempt to excuse the actions of a murderer, but we have a responsibility to seek an explanation for their madness. Everyone has a story.

Unequivocally, the stories of these young suspects begin at home: with the presence of domestic violence and the absence of good fathers, with the presence of alcohol and drug misuse, and the absence of a safe family environment, with the presence of malevolent role models and the absence of positive alternatives, with the presence of trauma and the absence of hope. These are not simple problems and, barring miracles, they are not going to be resolved overnight – or in anything close to the kind of short-term timescales demanded in this impatient world of ours.

But, amid the chaos, there are fragments of hope. There are some remarkable families out there who, like the Kinsellas, have lived through these realities and some amazing practitioners, charities and community organisations who know and understand what they're doing. We need to listen to them, we need to have the courage of our convictions and we need to invest heavily in the things that actually work. We need to do this in the knowledge that we may not see the full fruits of our labours for ten, twenty or even thirty years. We need to do these things because they are the right things to do.

The alternative is to stand back, helpless, as the same grim narrative plays itself out again and again.

*

The reality is that I'm willing to try pretty much anything to keep young people safe. It's a fact that leads to one of the more surreal experiences of my professional life. I find myself sitting in a well-appointed meeting room in Camden Lock, at the London headquarters of MTV. I'm with Patrick, my good friend who runs the brilliant youth charity XLP, and we're in the company of some high-powered people from the world of entertainment.

Not being part of the usual MTV demographic (too old and far too boring), I would be hard pressed to describe myself as a regular viewer, but I did once see an episode of an enjoyably daft programme called *Pimp My Ride*. The premise of the show was simple: take a clapped-out car belonging to a member of Joe Public and turn it into a souped-up version of something altogether more eye-catching. And it had set me wondering: could you take the idea and give it some soul and a social conscience? Find a bigger vehicle and turn it into something that would actually be of benefit and use to the community?

I'd made a slow start until I found myself in a small queue at Toronto airport, talking to the complete stranger lining up in front of me. Turned out he was English. Turned out he was someone important at MTV. So I pitched him the idea. Funny how these things work out.

One thing led to another and now we're here, with a group of people who appear to be actually listening to our madcap idea. Word becomes deed, and not too long after our meeting the programme makers are taking a decommissioned Met riot van and turning it into a mobile recording studio with all the bells and whistles. It will be a youth club on wheels, a place where young people can learn the art and craft of making music and where they can record their own songs. It makes for good TV, but far more importantly it provides a priceless resource that will be used by XLP on London's streets and estates for years to come.

I love the symbolism: taking a vehicle that most street-wise youngsters would run a mile from and turning it into something they might actually run towards. All it took was an idea and a coalition of the concerned who could make it work. EMI, that great old record company, put up much of the cash that made it happen and made it sustainable. And so I find myself at the programme launch event, dressed in full uniform and facing the flashing cameras in the company of a DJ called Westwood and a rapper called Chipmunk. Just like any other day at the office.

*

People are, by far, our most valuable resource and providing high-quality training for them should be seen as an investment, not a cost. Sadly, all too often, that ideal isn't borne out in reality. Training is becoming something of a 'Cinderella' part of the organisation, with fewer and fewer resources allocated to it and an increasing reliance on computer-based delivery that gives a bad impression of good development for our officers and staff. The situation is nowhere near good enough and I want to do something about it.

I put together a three-hour session for every officer on the borough. Over the course of several weeks, Adrian and I, together with our Borough Commander, meet with them in groups of about thirty at a time.

Locard's Principle has remained a source of significant inspiration over the years and I give the training the title 'Every Contact Matters' in a conscious nod to the old scientist and his remarkable idea. The thing I really want to focus on is the way in which we go about our duties: how we behave, the standards we set and maintain, how we treat people, how we treat one another.

We show the teams a series of interviews we've filmed with local people and, in particular, with local victims of crime. We'd sought out both those who'd had good experiences of the police in Islington and those who hadn't. We'd asked them to be completely honest with us. Their messages were immensely important and I wanted everyone to hear them.

There are some things we do brilliantly, like responding to emergencies or caring for victims in the immediate aftermath of serious incidents and showing immense courage in confronting violent and dangerous criminals. And we hear the stories of people whose lives have been changed very much for the better as a consequence of what we've done for them. But, equally, there are some things we do less well, such as keeping people updated about the progress of investigations and the ways in which some of us behave towards the public some of the time. What we do matters. How we do it matters just as much. Every contact matters.

*

All the while, the urgent reality of knife crime remains and spurs me on. I'm in north London, caught up in a conversation with an edgy young man. He pulls up his shirt and shows me a mess of old knife scars, criss-crossing his torso. I've never seen anything like it and the police have been oblivious to the origins of every single one of them.

Experience suggests that, the more vulnerable or marginalised a victim, the more likely it is that a crime will go unreported. It's an observation that applies to youth violence, to domestic violence, to rape, to child sexual exploitation, to human trafficking. And these are the things that ought to keep us awake at night.

*

I have other responsibilities, too. Tonight, Arsenal are hosting Barcelona in the Champions League and I have the responsibility of being the police Match Commander. It would be fair to say, though, that my pre-game preparation hasn't been ideal.

Two days ago I was in day surgery at Guy's Hospital, subjecting myself to the unspeakable indignities of 'the snip'. Having become a dad for the third time – the glorious joys of Emily Grace – it had seemed like the grown-up and responsible thing to do. Plus, I realised that I now had more children than I had hands and I recognised that I was more tired than I had ever been in my life.

I had made the choice to go for the local anaesthetic ('Man up,' I told myself) and it was an option I ought to have questioned from the moment I stripped naked and slipped into the backless hospital gown. The operating theatre was freezing cold, both of the nurses staring intently at my terrified vitals were female and the only man present apart from me was armed with an extremely sharp knife. What on earth was I thinking?

Fast forward forty-eight hours and I'm in the control room at Arsenal, surrounded by colleagues and club officials, and just beginning to realise that I probably ought to have allowed a little longer for the post-op recovery. The reality is that I'm starting to experience a significant degree of distress in the downstairs department. I'm wearing an NHS-issue 'support' that has to be at least three sizes too small and my sense of eye-watering discomfort is growing by the minute. My only consolation is the fact that I've got a highly experienced team around me and, as the policing operation gets under way and my professional responsibilities come to the fore, they give me an armchair ride. This turns out to be a very good thing as, within a few minutes of kick-off, I find that I'm no longer able to stand up. I do my best to keep my thoughts on the actual task in hand and when I'm not watching the crowd or the CCTV screens I find myself, just like everyone else, mesmerised by Messi.

The game itself passes without incident, at least from a policing point of view, and the ground empties. Just as we're thinking about closing down for the evening – and I'm wondering how I'm going to manage my bow-legged journey home – there's a flurry of activity on the opposite side of the stadium, up on one of the TV gantries. A call comes through on the club's radio system. Paramedics required. One of the cameramen was packing away his gear and collapsed. Just dropped to the ground, apparently. Everyone responds immediately and help is with him quickly.

From the control room we can see the whole eerie scene being played out about 400 yards away from us. I can make out people, but not faces. I can see the paramedic kneeling over the poor man. I can see his green-sleeved arms moving up and down in urgent repetition as he administers the chest compressions. Images without sound.

And I see a man die. Not for the first time; not for the last time. His loved ones will be getting that desperate knock on the door in the next hour or so.

All over the country, every day of the year, private tales of grief are being told. And police officers are so often a part of the telling.

✳

Reports come through of a gang rape. There can't be many more heinous offences. A group of teenage boys have somehow got access to a flat and they've prepared it in advance. Everything is premeditated. Their unsuspecting young target is lured inside and repeatedly raped, by one boy after another. It is an utter violation of the most horrifying kind and an act of monumental wickedness. At the end of an ordeal beyond comprehension, they just throw her out onto the street, before cleaning the location in an attempt to remove every last trace of their vile crime.

As is always the way with serious cases of this kind, the investigation will be passed on to a specialist team and I will very quickly lose track of what happens to the girl and her attackers. The world hurtles on and the crimes just keep coming.

*

Each year at Hendon, the Met holds a Service of Remembrance for fallen colleagues. This year, I have the duty and honour of representing the borough.

As we gather in front of the Memorial Garden and the military band plays Elgar's *Nimrod*, it's all that this officer in tunic and white gloves can do to hold himself together. Greater love hath no one than to lay their lives down.

During the course of my policing life, far too many of my colleagues have left home for work, never to return. These are the names of those Met officers who have been killed in the execution of their duty since I joined in September 1992 (source: the Police Roll of Honour Trust):

PC Michael Perry.
Died 18 April 1993, aged 36.
Killed when his patrol car crashed while responding to a 999 call.

PC Noel Frick.
Died 23 July 1993, aged 48.
Killed in an accident while on motorcycle surveillance duty.

PC Patrick Dunne.
Died 20 October 1993, aged 44.
Shot dead when responding to the sound of gunfire in the street.

PC Thomas Need.
Died 13 November 1993, aged 26.
Killed in an accident while on motorcycle surveillance duty.

Sergeant Derek Robertson QGM.
Died 9 February 1994, aged 39.
Stabbed and killed while attempting to arrest a suspect at a post-office robbery.

PC Michael Tring.
Died 26 September 1994, aged 31.
Fatally injured in a police car crash while responding to an assistance call.

PC Matthew Parsonson.
Died 7 October 1994, aged 27.
Fatally injured in a police car crash while responding to a call for help.

PC Phillip Walters.
Died 18 April 1995, aged 28.
Shot and fatally wounded while trying to arrest a violent suspect.

PC George Hammond.
Died 13 December 1995, aged 58.
Died as a result of stab wounds sustained during an arrest in 1985.

PC Stephen Williams.
Died 16 March 1996, aged 42.
Killed in a motorcycle accident while making security visits.

PC Nina MacKay.
Died 24 October 1997, aged 25.
Stabbed and killed after forcing entry into a flat to arrest a violent man.

PC Kulwant Singh Sidhu.
Died 25 October 1999, aged 24.
Killed when he fell through a glass skylight while chasing suspects.

PC Anthony Haines.

Died 14 March 2001, aged 42.

Fatally injured in a police car crash while responding to an emergency call.

PC Paul Johnson.

Died 20 June 2002, aged 35.

Fatally injured in a motorcycle accident while on patrol.

DC Nigel Syder.

Died 27 August 2002, aged 39.

Fatally injured in a motorcycle accident while on surveillance duty.

PC Christian Parker.

Died 27 November 2002, aged 29.

Fatally injured in a police car crash while responding to an emergency call.

PC Christopher Roberts.

Died 26 December 2007, aged 47.

Died of heart failure after arresting a violent man at a domestic disturbance.

PC Gary Toms.

Died 17 April 2009, aged 37.

Fatally injured on 11 April while attempting to arrest suspects escaping in a vehicle.

DC Adele Cashman.
Died 5 November 2012, aged 30.
*Collapsed while chasing two robbery suspects and later died
in hospital.*

PC Andrew Duncan.
Died 21 September 2013, aged 47.
*Died from injuries sustained after being struck by a
speeding vehicle that he had attempted to stop the previous
day.*

These are giants on whose shoulders we stand.

*

I continue to do my bit as a negotiator, and it continues to be
both challenging and rewarding.

It's the middle of the afternoon, and a male armed with a
weapon has barricaded himself into a ground-floor flat on an
estate up near Finsbury Park. His female partner is trapped
inside the address with him. I'm not on call but I am nearby,
so I offer to lend a hand.

By the time I get to the scene, all the cordons are in and the
TSG have surrounded the address. A group of three officers are
standing at a wooden gate ten feet or so from the front door.
They have positioned themselves behind a set of long shields
and one of them has managed to get the suspect involved in
an intermittent exchange of words. Our middle-aged man is
standing in the kitchen, to the left of the front door as we look
at it. The small window above the sink is open, making the
conversation possible. But it doesn't make it easy.

He is all over the place: calm then frantic, quiet then ranting, predictable then erratic, listening then paying no attention whatsoever. He's holding a large knife.

The TSG PC is doing a cracking job trying to talk to him, so I just listen in and offer the occasional whispered suggestion. It's not immediately clear whether the knifeman is high on something or suffering from some form of mental illness. The sad reality is probably some combination of the two. And there seems to be no clear explanation for the events of today, no apparent reason for the stand-off. We can see his partner inside the flat and she seems to be unharmed. We will need an emergency plan in case things escalate rapidly and she is placed at immediate risk of harm but, for now, we seem to have all the time in the world.

The flat sits in a natural amphitheatre on the estate, surrounded by embankments and raised walkways. An inevitable crowd gathers, looking down on every move, listening to every word, wondering what will happen next. It looks as though there are hundreds of them and this is evidently more diverting than the usual daily routine. They don't take sides. They can see the knife. They can hear us being reasonable, asking him to put it down and give himself up. It must be apparent to even the most partial observers that we're trying to do the right thing. So they just watch and wait. We wait too, building up a rapport, persuading, cajoling, talking him out.

He relents in the end and agrees to our requests. He is told to come to the front door with his hands above his head. Officers approach him carefully and handcuff him behind his back. He is barefoot, so I send one of the PCs inside to get him a pair of shoes. We help him into them as colleagues check that his partner is OK. As he is led quietly to the back of the van that has reversed up close to the address, a ripple of applause breaks out among those looking on. Show over.

*

There's a whole world beyond the capital and I complete the additional training needed to take my place on the international negotiator call-out list. And I find myself caught up in stories that can't be told: stories without happy endings. Back in London, the calls keep coming too.

XI. *Markham Square*

Aside from at the inquest, I have never spoken or written in public about what happened at Markham Square in May 2008. For as long as the possibility remains that doing so will cause distress or pain to those who grieve for the loss of their loved one in that quiet corner of west London, I never will.

All I will say is this: there are days and then there are days: days that pass amiably; days that fade happily into the memory, blurring among themselves; wedding days and birthdays; high days and holy days. And then there are the other days – the ones that sear themselves into your very being and remain.

At Markham Square, I lived through one of those days. I was a hostage negotiator at a major armed siege and a man died on my watch. I was there when the fatal police shots were fired. I was the last living soul to hold a conversation with him.

I mention it now only to make sense of some of what follows.

XII. *The Seventeenth Floor*

It's another grainy, grey north London afternoon. I'm catching up with the team in the borough control room when local officers come through on the radio, requesting the assistance of hostage negotiators. They've got a man high up in a tower block, threatening to jump.

It's been more than six months since Markham Square and I've not been out on a negotiator job since. I'm not on call now, but I'm almost certainly the nearest trained negotiator to the location. I don't give it a second thought: instinct and adrenalin and that sense of duty combine and compel me. 'Are you ready to save a life?'

The flats in question are a short shout away from the Emirates Stadium – home of Arsenal – and, apparently, the man is on the seventeenth floor. It's a hell of a long way down from there.

A swift blue-light run later, I arrive at the location and take the lift to the sixteenth floor. Always stop on the level below; never let the doors open directly into the unknown;

give yourself time and space to think and prepare for whatever is to come. The stairwell between sixteen and seventeen is full of PCs, talking in whispers and standing by. None of them has much in the way of information they can give me, but local residents have been told to stay indoors and the area around the block has been cordoned off.

I head through the door on seventeen, onto the communal landing, and into a thin space between life and death. I take a deep breath. How do you start a conversation with a man on the edge?

I look to my left, absorbing the scene. At the far end of the landing – past an assortment of faceless front doors – there's a huge window, stretching almost from floor to ceiling. Standing beside it is a uniformed PC and, on the other side of the glass, is a young man dressed in casual clothing. For reasons I can't even begin to comprehend, the window can be opened from the inside – allowing the young man to climb outside and close it to a crack behind him. He's now standing on a ledge that can be no more than about three inches wide, holding onto the metal frame with his left hand.

And so it begins. The PC, holding a mobile phone, looks at me. All I have to offer him and the stranger on the other side are my wits and my words. Our man is from Eastern Europe and English is far from being his first language. The PC has managed to get an interpreter on the phone and is doing the best he can in an almost impossibly challenging set of circumstances. As I approach, the man takes the phone from the PC, says something to the interpreter and passes it back through the tiny gap in the window. I step forward hesitantly to take it and, as I do so, take in the vast distance between us and the ground. Immediately, I regret having looked. In any other context, the views across Islington would be spectacular, but not right now. Something doesn't feel right. I'm unsettled in a way that I've never experienced before.

I speak on the phone and then give it back for the translation. The simple act of handing it over is hold-your-breath-and-shatter-your-nerves stuff. Communicating like this is impossible, and exceptionally dangerous. I dispense with the mobile and decide that broken English, however difficult, is the least bad option we have.

I listen to what I can make out of his story. He's recently arrived in the UK and is having trouble finding a job and a place to stay. The struggle has evidently taken him to the end of himself. It's just desperately sad – though I can work out no reason why he's chosen this particular day and this particular block of flats. As he talks, I let my back slide down the bare concrete wall and sit on the hard floor – an attempt to put him at his ease. We continue our fractured conversation, with me trying my best to reason and reassure, and him trying to reveal his agony – each of us trying to understand the other. We are two complete strangers thrown together in this moment and it's impossible not to feel responsible for whatever might happen next.

As we fumble words between us, my natural and usual optimism continues to fade. In my mind's eye, I begin to imagine the moment he jumps. Or perhaps he slips. The unwelcome and desperately unnerving thoughts take hold and start to play on a loop in my head.

I am completely on my own. It's just me on the landing now. The PC has retreated and everyone else is tucked away on the stairs and on the floor below. It all depends on me. And, suddenly, I find myself back in Markham Square.

Without any prior warning, the memories of that bleak day come flooding back and I am completely wrong-footed. Before Markham Square, I hadn't had a single negative negotiating experience to look back on. I had always been able to play a part in saving the lives that had been hanging in the balance. I'd been called on and I'd done my bit. But last time out changed everything. It ended badly and now it seems to me that the chances are this one will as well. Mentally and emotionally, I'm trying to prepare myself for what is becoming inevitable. I'm not doing so well. But there is no option except to keep going.

Out of the corner of my eye, I see the hand of a colleague appearing round the base of the door frame – placing a tape recorder on the floor. I want to punch whoever it is that thinks this is a good time to be mucking about with recording equipment. I understand the desire to capture what's being said – not least for the benefit of any post-incident review – but, just at this moment, it feels as though the smallest thing could be the last thing.

My man remains on the other side of the window. Time passes agonisingly slowly – my mouth caught up in disjointed talk, my ears straining to understand, my mind distracted by desperate possibilities. I am a muddled mixture of compassion and hidden desperation. I don't think I'll be able to cope if he goes.

Tick, tick, tick...

There can never be time limits on a negotiation: things will always take as long as they take when the job is to save a life. But after an age – and entirely contrary to the sense of despair that has taken hold – I hear him saying that he wants to come back in.

I can't remember how we got there; I just know that we did. But there's no sense of relief. He's on the wrong side of a window that hinges in the middle and I have no idea how to get him back in. The ledge is terrifyingly narrow and, beyond it, there is just empty space and gravity.

Tick, tick, tick...

It's all in the balance, and to lose him now would certainly be more than I can bear. I inch towards him. The window is jammed.

Shit.

I'm terrified that I'm going to push too hard, terrified that I'm going to push him off.

Shit, shit, shit...

By now, I can barely breathe. I feel physically sick. Oh please, God...

I work gently on the catch from my side, like a nervous father handling a newborn for the first time. He works on the frame from his side – tiny movements with everlasting consequences. His life is in our two pairs of hands and I am scared beyond words. Somehow, though, we manage it and, suddenly, he's standing on the right side of the glass with solid floor under his feet. I could almost weep with relief.

No more than sixty seconds later, it begins to absolutely

sheet with rain – a downpour of truly biblical proportions. Goodness only knows what would have happened if he'd still been out there.

A group of PCs lead him away to whatever comes next – one of thousands of migrants who don't show up on the census or on any other kind of official record, one more member of London's hidden communities. I hope he does OK, that he manages to get back on his feet, that he doesn't find himself back here again.

As the rest of us head down the stairs, there's plenty of banter – the satisfaction and relief of a job well done. But I trail behind them, alone and lost in my thoughts. This particular happy ending has somehow passed me by and I find that I am haunted by the prospect of what could have been. I can still see him fall.

These are unfamiliar emotions and I have no idea what to do with them. I'm troubled and I don't understand. I'm bothered and I don't know why. But I don't talk to anyone. Not even to Bear. What would I say?

I wait for the raw feelings to pass and try to bury the images of what might have happened up there on the seventeenth floor somewhere beyond my mind's immediate view. I'm needed back at work.

XIII. *Borough Command*

The mobile buzzes in my pocket and I step out of a meeting to take the call. It's the Met's Director of HR telling me that I've passed the chief superintendent's assessment process. He seems genuinely pleased for me, but I'm not quite sure I believe that I've got through. A few minutes later, my phone goes again. This time it's the Assistant Commissioner with the same good news. They can't both be wrong.

I take a few moments to absorb it all and then ring Bear. I feel proud and utterly delighted. In four or five months' time, I will take my first full operational command in Camden. Even after all this time and despite a few grey hairs, I still look a little too young to be in charge.

I turned forty earlier in the year and, eighteen years into my policing career, I'm in the prime of my working life. The deep unease I felt in the aftermath of the incident on the seventeenth floor appears to have subsided and I feel in good shape. I'm looking forward to the next adventure and I'm determined to be the best chief superintendent I can be. At the same time, I'm also trying to be the best husband and father – the very best person – that I can be.

From time to time, Bear tells me that she finds it exhausting. She suggests that she and the girls can't keep up with the relentless standards and pace that I'm setting for myself. But I don't understand what she means, so I don't hear what she's trying to tell me. She wants me to slow down, just at the point when my policing journey is picking up real pace and intensity. I ought to have paid much closer attention.

*

I once heard it suggested that the job of Borough Commander in the Met is the most challenging to be found anywhere in the public sector. The observation had been made, not by a police officer, but by the chief executive of a London local authority. Well, I can't speak for everyone else, but it's certainly the most challenging job I've ever had. It's also the most fulfilling, humbling, inspiring, daunting, shattering, rewarding and soul-stirring job I've ever had.

As the Borough Commander, all roads lead to your door. They come from every direction – and it's all about people. First come the officers, staff and volunteers I serve alongside. Some of them are idiots, capable of all manner of stupidity. But most of them are heroes. Some of them are pompous, self-important buffoons. But most of them would go to the ends of the earth for you. Some of them are idle, work-shy lumberers. But most of them would, without a second thought, pour themselves out on your behalf. Some of them are economical with the truth and some hold a view of the world that no decent person would share. Some are quite simply corrupt and have no place among us. But most of them are extraordinary – among the finest men and women you could ever hope to meet.

It's people who make places safer. It's people who respond to calls. It's people who catch criminals and comfort victims. It's people who understand the things you cannot put a price on, but that we cannot afford to be without, like that precious and old-fashioned thing called duty. It's people, stupid.

My job, it seems to me, is to get out of their way, to enable them to get on and do what they do to the very best of their abilities. Inevitably, a minority of them will become a source of endless weariness and they will take a hugely dispropor-tionate amount of my time and energy. But the rest will be a source of endless pride and inspiration: the bold ones, the compassionate ones, the courageous ones, the relentless ones, the injured ones, the funny ones, the steady ones, the ones who will not shy away, the ones who understand the privilege of public service.

One of the greatest delights of my working life is to cel-ebrate their bravery and brilliance, to share their personal and professional success. One of the greatest sorrows is to share their pain.

Then there are the people we serve, the vulnerable and the victims in particular. They are, in so many respects, our reason for being and I care enormously about the ways in which we regard and treat them. Dr Locard is still right. Every contact really does leave a trace. There is, too, a wider population, those who may not have much direct contact with us, but who still have an interest in what we do:

Londoners who care about their communities and who are prepared to challenge and support us in equal measure.

Then there are the bosses. Some of them are brilliant: professional and highly experienced, they trust and empower and encourage us to get on with it. Some of them are marginally less brilliant, particularly those who appear only to be interested in the numbers, who seem to care more about pie charts than they do about people and who appear to be in it for no one other than themselves, forever with an eye on the next career opportunity. They too take up a disproportionate amount of my time and energy. At times, they suck the very life out of me and I am left reflecting ruefully on the endless differences between bad management and good leadership.

And, of course, there are the politicians. Irrespective of party or persuasion, the best of them are outstanding people: public servants for whom it really is all about their constituents and the greater good. They are, genuinely, a pleasure to work with. But the worst of them are almost unbearable – triumphs of soundbite over substance, of expedience over conscience, of short-termism and self-interest over service. Like the bad managers, they make my job harder than it needs to be.

*

I begin my first day in charge at Camden with the early-turn parade at Holborn Police Station. I dislike getting up at five in the morning more than I can say, but I want to be where they are.

The breadth and the depth of the responsibility we share are just extraordinary: more than a thousand officers and staff, tens of thousands of reported crimes every year and goodness knows how many unreported, five police stations, a local resident population of well over 200,000, swelled by the daily surge of commuters and tourists, a large chunk of the West End, three of the busiest rail terminals in Europe, the richest and the poorest side by side, all the world in one place. And our part in the midst of it all is to venture where most wouldn't and do what most couldn't. It's one heck of a job.

*

I once heard mention of an unnamed American general who was asked for his view on the secrets of great leadership. His answer was a straightforward one: 'Drink more coffee.'

I'm not actually a fan of the bean, but I take the point. It seems to me that the simple secret is to spend time with people: getting to know and understand them, building relationships of mutual respect and trust with them, letting them know that they matter. It's about having meetings without agendas. That's how I will spend much of my time at Camden: with my senior team, with the late-turn van driver and her colleagues on the response team, with the crime squad in their untidy office at Kentish Town, with police staff colleagues and Special Constables, with local neighbourhood PCs, with the Community Safety Unit DCs carrying goodness knows how many domestic violence investigations. I walk the floors, wander through offices and pull up a chair in the canteen, taking time with the people who matter. I also spend a great deal of time with Camden council, with community leaders and charities and businesses and with people, young and old, who live and work in my part of town.

I take the 'Every Contact Matters' training I developed at Islington and now, as Borough Commander, introduce it to my new officers and staff members. I want to allow time for honest conversations, for people to have the freedom to ask difficult questions, and I want them to know that what they do is important to me. That they are important to me.

I show my teams some new films we've made, including one in which Brooke Kinsella tells the story of Ben's murder with astonishing power and dignity. In her family's darkest days, the police were there for them. We couldn't bring Ben back, but we could offer comfort and reassurance, we could catch his killers and we could ensure that justice was served.

But history just keeps on repeating itself. In April 2011, a few months after I arrive in the borough, twenty-two-year-old Milad Golmakani is knifed to death, stabbed fourteen times in the back and neck. Another young life. Another round of hopeless headlines. Another shattered family. His teenage friend is also stabbed, but survives. This cannot keep happening. What was the promise I made to George Kinsella?

The scene of Milad's murder is a children's playground in a quiet corner of Kilburn, north London. The suspects for the killing – all teenagers – are believed to have connections with a street gang known as the 'QC'. Their territory is around Queens Crescent in Kentish Town. As the Murder Team go after the main suspects, we go after the rest of the gang.

Queens Crescent runs along the southern edge of a fairly typical north London estate: a mixture of high- and low-rise, with a concrete football pitch and a few patches of green.

There's a community centre and a small parade of shops, complete with those two seeming staples of London's poorer neighbourhoods: the takeaway and the betting shop. It's one of those places where you can, on occasions, sense a change in the atmosphere after dark.

The fact is that the overwhelming number of those living there are good people – a mixture of families and hard-working folk, minding their own business. But the dealers have taken over: predatory criminals, many of them not even from the local area, have settled on the estate and its surrounds as the place to ply their trade. Drugs and violence cast long shadows. Most of the dealers are linked to the QC gang and are implicated in a string of other violent incidents prior to Milad's death.

Conventional police tactics just haven't worked. As soon as a uniform patrol ventures anywhere near the estate, the dealers and their runners simply vanish, with the geography of the area providing any number of escape routes and hiding places. Advantage them. So we launch Operation Home Run. The focus is on the deployment of Test Purchase Officers (TPOs), a uniquely brave and unconventional breed. They work undercover, adopting the persona of a drug user and getting in among the dealers to secure evidence of them in the act. We have two very simple aims: to give a neighbourhood back to its community and to lock up some very dangerous criminals.

Each target is identified and given an operational pseudonym – in this case the names of American baseball teams – and officers begin to build an overwhelming case against each one of them. The main man is Yankee. He and his cohort have no idea what we're doing or what's coming.

The evidence gathering takes a number of weeks, with officers working long hours in difficult and sometimes very dangerous conditions. One of the TPs is robbed by one of the targets. He emerges from the encounter unscathed, with irrefutable evidence of another serious crime secured. The case just keeps getting stronger. Advantage us.

Eventually, we have everything we need and we move to the arrest phase. I want us to make a statement: first to the dealers, that they will not be tolerated; second to the local community, that we are for them and will remain so. More than 200 officers take part on the day. We hold a covert briefing in a Territorial Army training centre in another borough, and then we wait. We can't go until the majority of our targets take up their usual pitches. After seemingly endless delays, the call comes from the main OP that we're good to go. TSG officers pile into the back of a number of nondescript box vans and, slowly, they encircle the estate. They will be followed in by local community officers, who will reassure and provide explanations for local residents and businesses. We've also got the press with us and the lead council member for community safety.

I hear the instruction from control relayed over the radio: 'Go, go, go.' Adrenalin and anticipation coincide. This had better work. And it does.

I'm sixty seconds behind the main strike in another car and I don't get to see the full deployment effect, but I imagine it looks pretty impressive: uniformed officers pouring out of the back of trucks and forming a human dragnet that covers every alley and stairwell in the immediate neighbourhood. Our targets are going nowhere.

As I make my way through the police cordons that are now in place on the edge of the estate, I'm approached by a local resident who wants to shake my hand. Others follow. People are genuinely grateful. It's a great feeling: this is looking like being one of those precious days when you realise that you might actually be making a real difference to the lives of decent people. Then comes an unexpected turn of events.

As I'm walking along one of the estate roads inside the cordon with my Staff Officer and the councillor, one of the Home Run spotters rushes up to me and points out a white male, early twenties, no more than about twenty yards ahead of us. 'That's Yankee,' he says breathlessly. And it is. I, of course, would have walked straight past him – oblivious to his significance in the case. Thank heavens for good street cops who know what they're doing.

So I go up to Yankee and, because he doesn't know what we know and because he's not carrying, he's happy enough to stop and talk. I make a quick phone call to control to confirm who I have and the strength of the evidence against him. And, somewhat unexpectedly, I find myself as the arresting officer. It's not the sort of thing that Borough Commanders are renowned for doing, as making arrests is, generally speaking, the preserve of the PCs, and I've not been in this position for quite some time. But I manage to remember the wording of the caution. Yankee still hasn't got a clue what's going on as we put him in the back of the van.

'Control, Control. Active Message.' It's the Crime Squad DS on the radio. Known to everyone as Muddy – with the surname 'Waters', what else were people ever going to call him? – he's one of the best detectives I've had the pleasure of working with. 'Active Message' is meant to signify something important or urgent. All other units stand by.

Control: 'Unit with the Active Message – go ahead.'

Muddy again: 'The Borough Commander has arrested the main target; I repeat, the Borough Commander has arrested the main target.'

Sometimes you just have to laugh.

*

I'm told that Yankee was later heard talking to his girl-friend on the custody phone, bawling his eyes out. The team had done their job. The evidence against him and his co-conspirators was overwhelming and he was going to jail.

On 27 January 2012, in the case of R v McVicar and others at the Crown Court, His Honour Judge Hillen was concluding proceedings: 'I do not turn from this case without commending the officers who have been involved in this extensive investigation. It is clear to me that this operation was extremely effective and that this has substantially reduced the criminal and anti-social behaviour in the area . . .'

I am endlessly stirred by what the Met's people accomplish. But the fact remains that we were too late for Milad Golmakani. Four teenagers, all with connections to Queens Crescent, are later convicted of his murder.

*

In addition to the violent crimes involving young people, domestic violence continues to trouble me deeply. I'm talking to a local youth worker, employed by an exceptional charity and working in some of the borough's secondary schools. She tells some powerful stories.

On one occasion, she headed into a local girls' school to meet a group of teenagers. She was looking for a way to get the conversation started and, with an all-female audience, she settled on the subject of relationships. She started with what she thought was a simple question: 'What makes for a good relationship?'

To her surprise, she was met with complete silence. No one said a word – until finally, one teenage girl spoke up. 'One where he doesn't hit you,' she said.

Pause and think about her answer for a moment. Every time I've related that brief story to people, I never fail to be stunned by her reply. Even if you were to try to argue that her views were not broadly representative of her peer group, the fact that any young woman is growing up in our society and the sum total of her aspirations for a relationship is the hope of avoiding violence... It's a horrifying thought.

*

Families are the foundations on which communities are built, for better or for worse. Policing provides a haunting insight into the latter half of that old vow – into what is described by a friend and colleague in the local Youth Offending Service as 'the intergenerational transference of harm'.

If you want to understand why a young person might join

a gang, look first at his family setting. If you want to find out why a young person is a repeat truant from school, begin at home. If you want to understand the terrifying growth in child and adolescent mental-health problems, take a look behind the front door. If you want to understand how a young person turns into an uncontrollable ball of rage, look at where he came from. If you want to even begin to comprehend how one eleven-year-old boy could take the life of another, ask about the violence he's witnessed and experienced growing up. All roads lead to home.

Camden is one of the first local authorities to take on the Government's 'Troubled Families' initiative. The thinking goes that a relatively small number of families place a disproportionately high demand on public services and resources. And no one agency has the monopoly on responding to that demand.

It's true, of course. The house that the police get called to several times a week is the same one being visited with increasing regularity by Social Services and the Education Welfare Officer. The council's Anti-Social Behaviour Team are likely to be preparing an application or two for court and several members of the household will have been identified by the local GP's surgery as being a source of significant concern. There are older family members who are third-generation unemployed and younger ones who are currently in Feltham Young Offenders' Institution.

Locally, I'm impressed by the willingness of senior partners – from the council, from health, from education and beyond – to tackle the issues head on and to consider some very different approaches. There is no attempt by anyone to hide from past failings.

A small number of us are given unrestricted access to the case files relating to some of the families in question. I walk into the room where the paperwork is being stored and find tables full of endless binders that are several inches thick. Most families have more than one. It's pretty devastating stuff. What the contents reveal are repeated cycles of endless brokenness and complexity on the part of the families, and repetitions of failed intervention on the part of the state. Thousands of hours and hundreds of thousands of pounds seem to have been invested for no discernible benefit or change: different agencies, at different times, attempting to intervene and stumbling into frustrations, dead ends, intransigence and one another.

Most people, for the most part, have been doing the very best that they can, but it feels almost impossible – not least because the families in greatest need of help and support are among the least likely to ask for or accept it. I don't feel any sense of judgement about them. I don't have the right, and being a parent can be damn hard work, but it can also be one of the most glorious responsibilities of adult life. There certainly aren't many entries on the list of things that matter more.

I have any number of failings as a dad. I can be grumpy and impatient and frustrated and downright unreasonable. But I am learning how to say sorry to my girls – and to my wife – and to comfort and protect and nurture and guide them to the very best of my abilities. Loving them is the most important duty I will ever have.

Policing continues to reveal the desperate ways in which things can turn out when love is set aside.

*

As the Troubled Families conversation continues, I find myself in a meeting room at the town hall, looking at one of the simplest and most powerful pieces of analysis I have ever seen. It's in the form of a single piece of handwritten flipchart paper, set out like a family tree, to show three or four generations of one local family. Everyone is included in the picture – from the oldest to the soon-to-be-born. They are shown by an abbreviation rather than their full name, with an additional designation, in red pen, to identify those individuals who have been a victim of, or exposed to, domestic violence. The entire page is just a sea of red. Domestic violence at almost every point, in every generation.

*

In addition to my day job in Camden, I take my regular turn on the superintendents' night-duty rota. There are certain responsibilities in law that can only be fulfilled by someone of the rank of superintendent and above – such as the authorisation of a person's detention in police custody beyond the initial twenty-four-hour time limit. When I first joined, you needed to wake a senior officer up at home to get that sort of thing done and it just makes more sense to have one of us awake and closer to hand.

So, for three nights at a time, I'm the senior officer on duty for half of London. And it turns out that the things I've seen in the places where I've worked are the things that are common to most, if not all, London boroughs. I see patterns repeat themselves right across the capital: domestic violence, alcohol-fuelled violence, serious youth violence, knives and guns, drugs, organised crime, the abuse of the vulnerable, the impact of mental illness, the stories of endless distress, in this city that is my home.

Tonight, I'm covering London north of the Thames. Calls come in to shots fired in Camden and I'm not far away.

As I arrive on scene, the victim is lying by the side of the road, surrounded by officers, paramedics and endless rolls of bandages. He's a notorious local gang leader and an enemy of the QC. Just at the moment, he's making a lot of noise, and with good reason. He has a serious shotgun wound to his left leg. He will survive, but for now, he's a right mess.

The paramedic is asking him how bad the pain is, on a scale of one to ten. 'Ten,' is his strangled scream.

A suspect vehicle has been seen making off from the scene, but we don't have a number plate for it. The cordons are in and urgent house-to-house enquiries are underway. Somewhere out there, we have an unknown suspect armed with a shotgun. And an evident willingness to use it.

Muddy is the night duty DS. He arrives at the scene and I'm pleased to see him. He costs me a fortune in overtime, but he's worth every shilling. After a couple of minutes, he spots me and pulls me to one side: 'He's done that to himself.'

'What?'

'Shot himself – by accident . . . I reckon he was in the car with his mates and it's gone off accidentally. You can guess what they were on their way to do.'

He's been here for less time than me and he's already come up with this working theory. I was miles behind.

Muddy is absolutely right. Weeks of investigation later and the Shootings Team will be in agreement. We'll never prove it of course, but no one is in any doubt. The reality is that if he hadn't managed to shoot himself, he'd have shot someone else. And the cycle of violence goes on. Shootings, stabbings, glassings, full-blown Wild West punch-ups. Most of them over nothing.

*

Talking of punch-ups. We've got Camden Town on our patch: a brilliant, buzzing, cornucopia of colour and eccentricity, one that can be a complete nightmare to police when the booze is flowing freely. Fighting drunks as suspects, merry drunks as victims, drunks of every kind who demand endless police time and attention. And who, often as not, end up in hospital.

We set up Operation Numerus – a simple doubling of the number of uniforms on the streets on a Friday and Saturday night – just to keep a lid on it all. It's reasonably successful, but it comes at huge cost to the public purse and it leaves us with less capacity to deal with other problems and challenges. If you think buying alcohol is expensive, try putting a price on dealing with the fallout from people drinking too much of the stuff.

*

Some people behave badly when they've had too much to drink. Some venues are just run badly.

The Den is a nightclub on the edge of the West End. And it comes to my notice very early in my time at Camden, for all the wrong reasons. I've always had an open mind when it comes to pubs and clubs. I'm no puritan and I understand the importance of the late-night economy for local boroughs – and for London as a whole. For that reason, I've always been supportive professionally of licensed premises that are run safely and responsibly. But when they become associated with crime of every kind, I have an entirely different view.

That's the case with the Den. There are reports of GBH, Class A drug dealing, robbery and the rest – repeated evidence of endemic criminality associated directly with the venue. During my first eight months in Camden, no other licensed premises in the borough has been raised so frequently as a concern. In fact, no other licensed premises has really come close.

With colleagues from the Licensing Team – all of us in full uniform – I pay the place a visit late one Friday night. In the VIP section, my feet stick to the floor. We speak to staff and review the security arrangements. We later send in a Crime Prevention Design Advisor and I meet with the man who owns and runs the place to explain my extensive and growing concerns. We give them every opportunity to put things right. But the venue remains a menace.

It takes months and an awful lot of hard work but, eventually, we manage to close it down. I have no interest in spoiling a night out for people, but every interest in saving lives and in confronting the criminals who operate without regard for the rule of law or the safety of the public. The Den was a malignant, corrosive presence in the borough. Good riddance.

*

It's not just the Den, though. I stare at the grainy CCTV footage taken from the basement of another club in Camden Town. I watch the suspect cross the dance floor. I watch him walk silently behind the bar and make his way into the kitchen. Moments later, I see him reappear with a large knife in his hand. Off camera, he stabs an innocent young man to death. And so we are called. The following morning at the police station I sit with his brother and the group of friends who were there when he died. Their faces are blank and sleepless and disbelieving.

*

Violence and booze become recurring themes. Alcohol makes people vulnerable to predators.

I'm on night duty again and I'm out on patrol in central London. We get a call from a member of the public reporting a West End minicab driver who appears to be trying to kiss a resisting young woman in his vehicle. We're not far away and we've got a vehicle index. Northbound, Tottenham Court Road.

We're quickly behind it and we pull it over. The vehicle has two occupants: older male driver and a young female in the front passenger seat. My colleague takes a middle-aged, overweight man away from the vehicle and I get into the driver's seat to speak to the woman. She's in her early twenties, casually dressed, and she's had a hell of a lot to drink. As a consequence, she's not entirely coherent, but I manage to establish that, yes, he has tried to kiss her (and probably more besides). It was uninvited and entirely unwelcome.

I go round to the passenger side to let her out. She can barely stand up. I have to reach out to steady her as she stumbles.

He gets nicked for indecent assault and my first thought is the sincere hope that the eventual punishment will match the seriousness of the crime.

*

Neil is the borough's detective superintendent, responsible for overseeing the work of the local CID officers. He's a few years older than me and his son and daughter are grown up. It turns out he has a bit of parenting advice for me: 'Let me tell you the difference between raising boys and raising girls,' he says. 'With a boy, you've only got one willy to worry about; with a girl, there are millions of the bastards.'

He smiles, a thoroughly decent man pleased to have been able to pass on some wisdom to a younger colleague.

When Neil retires, Richard arrives as his replacement. He's old school and he's brilliant, with a big heart and a compelling sense of duty, and he loves a good story. His dad had retired as a detective superintendent and, between the two of them, Richard has more than fifty years' worth of yarns and tales to call on. He is quite willing to tell them all, particularly with a pint in front of him. He's good company and quickly becomes a good friend. We have different styles, but we care about the same things. We share the same ambitions – getting crime down, improving the service we give to victims and looking after the troops. We also share the same frustrations – the daily grind, meaningless meetings and certain bosses who don't seem to get it. Sometimes, it's just good to talk to someone who understands, who has been where you've been and seen the things you've seen.

As the Borough Commander, I'm the public face of policing in the local area and I'm at a community meeting, taking questions from the floor. Financially, times are tight and getting tighter. The public sector is really beginning to feel the squeeze of austerity. In times of plenty, policing benefited from extraordinary levels of investment. But everything is changing now. Which means choices and the need for some honest conversations. Because everything can't be a priority.

The next query comes from a man who has had his bicycle stolen. Big deal for him, but it feels to him as though it is less of a big deal to the police. Not unreasonably, he wants to know why. First thing to acknowledge is that any crime is significant for a victim, even if it's just because of the sheer inconvenience and cost involved in replacing something that's been taken. Often, of course, it's far more serious than that. Familiarity should never breed complacency among police officers.

I apologise to him, before explaining to him and the rest of the audience the reality of the economic situation and the consequent range of competing demands for police resources. It isn't that his crime doesn't matter to me – it really does – it's just that there are a number of other things that have to matter more. I acknowledge that I probably haven't told him what he wants to hear. But I have told him the truth. Somewhat to my surprise, he thanks me. He says it's the first straight answer he's been given on the subject. Now why should that be so hard to do?

*

One of the first things you're told about being a Borough Commander is that you're responsible for something called 'performance'. What this should mean is that you're responsible for pouring your professional heart and soul into doing whatever it takes to make a place safer and improving the policing service offered to the people who live, work and pass through there. It should mean that you're responsible for making a difference. But, if you're not careful, what it can actually turn into is the blind pursuit of arbitrary targets.

We're absolutely obsessed with numbers. Or, at least, most of the world seems to be. If it moves, measure it. If it doesn't move, measure it anyway. You never know, it might just move at some point in the future. Numbers take up far too much of my time as a Borough Commander, despite the fact that, in my experience, numbers don't actually make places safer. It's people who do that. As others have remarked before me, not everything that matters can be measured. And not everything that gets measured actually matters. Quite apart from anything else, there are all sorts of questions and concerns to be raised about the accuracy and reliability of the things we do add up and display in charts. Goodhart's Law sums it up pretty well: 'When a measure becomes a target, it ceases to be a good measure.'

And the undeniable experience – in policing and beyond – is that the imposition of targets has a tendency to skew behaviour. The pursuit of the target affects the integrity of the measure, and the danger is that we end up doing what's counted, rather than what counts. Policing is at least as much art as it is science and how on earth do you put a value on the additional time taken with an especially vulnerable victim?

Take the following two crime reports. The first is a burglary. A home-cinema system valued at five thousand pounds has been stolen. The victim is a middle-aged businessman who was at work when the crime was committed.

The second is also a burglary. Again, the value of the property taken is five thousand pounds. But in this case, the victim is an eighty-five-year-old woman living in sheltered accommodation. She was at home at the time and has lost her life savings – a biscuit tin full of cash, hidden under her bed.

On a bland spreadsheet, there's a real danger that these two crimes look the same. They share the same classification. The sum of money involved is the same. But don't try telling me that they're comparable offences. They're not. Not even close.

If all we do is count numbers, we miss what matters more. We miss the telling detail of each crime and the consequent impact on victims and communities. And that's just plain wrong. We should never waver from investing the greatest time, effort and resource in the crimes – and the criminals – that cause the greatest harm. And if that means certain other things getting less attention than some of us might like, then so be it.

Domestic violence has to matter more than shoplifting. Youth violence and knife crime have to matter more than the theft of a pushbike. Any crime that has a child or vulnerable person as its victim has to matter more than one that doesn't. We need to get beyond the recurring madness of 'hitting the target, but missing the point'.

Yes, there is an absolute need for scrutiny and accountability, together with a means of knowing whether we are getting better at what we do, but we have got to stop bowing at the altar of the number gods.

*

It's not just the performance figures that are giving me cause for concern. I'm sitting in my office at Holborn looking at a financial quote. It's for a plug, the sort that goes in a sink, rather than a socket. Apparently, we're missing one at Kentish Town and a replacement has been requested.

Why on earth am I bothering to look at this particular document? Because we're being asked to pay in excess of £90. For a plug. Well, actually, for four plugs, according to the paperwork I'm looking at. We have a contract with a private-sector supplier, as a consequence of which they seem to think it acceptable to charge whatever they like. In this case, a potential mark-up of somewhere in the region of 8,900 per cent. I promise you I haven't invented this.

They will tell you that they have to source the product; that they have to deliver it; that they have to fit it; that they have to cover their insurance. And so on. But I can buy one on the internet or on the high street for a pound, probably less if I shop around a bit.

It's a small story, but told to make a big point. This is public money and someone, somewhere is having a field day with it. I could tell you endless tales of the same sort: hundreds and thousands and millions of pounds spent on plugs and things right across policing and beyond. And I can't think of a single justification.

I don't doubt there's a dose of public-sector cluelessness in the negotiation of these contracts. And I suspect that there's no shortage of switched-on business people waiting to take advantage. Someone, somewhere needs to develop a financial conscience. But what do I know? I'm just Plod.

*

Each morning at work, I pick up the overnight reports – records of crimes and incidents from the past twenty-four hours. Whenever I hear that any of the PCs have been injured or been involved in something particularly testing or traumatic, I make a point of getting hold of them to check that they're OK. When their shifts allow, I invite them up to my office for a cuppa and a conversation. They tell me their stories – tales of horror and heartbreak and harm. In their own way, these have as much of an impact on me as the things I've seen and experienced first hand. I suppose it's a little like sitting alongside a chain smoker and filling your lungs with their fumes.

They tell me, for example, about the young student who was making her way home at the end of the day. Her clothes became caught in the wheels of a moving bus and she was dragged underneath. The driver was completely unaware of what was happening and kept going. The bus chewed her up and spat her out further up the road. Her body was so badly damaged that the first officers on scene thought that she must have fallen from an aeroplane at 30,000 feet.

I find it impossible to hear and imagine these things and to remain untouched by them.

*

London's burning.

It's the summer of 2011 and riots have broken out across the capital and beyond. The spark appears to have been the fatal police shooting of a man called Mark Duggan.

I happen to be in France with my family as Camden becomes one of those parts of London seriously affected. Buildings are also on fire within a short walk of our south London home. I sit, watching the live news feeds, feeling an unyielding sense of personal and professional frustration at not being able to take my place alongside my colleagues. I want to be there. I want to be involved. I want to do my bit.

We get back two days after the worst of it and I return to the aftermath in my borough. In the days that follow, London feels different. Having seen some of the worst that people can do, we now see the best, as local community members armed with brooms instead of bricks start the process of clearing up the mess. London seems to feel differently about its police officers too. Some of mine report being applauded down the street as they go about their duties. Rightly so. They have been working all the hours, snatching moments of sleep on the station floor before heading out for the next extended shift.

And the Met itself has, for now at least, set aside so much of what is unimportant: waste-of-time meetings and targets included. We have remembered what matters more: protecting the people of this great city and feeling proud of those we serve alongside.

Take, for example, the group of Camden officers who found themselves in the middle of the worst of it all. Their inspector tells a powerful story. They are in a marked carrier – one of the hastily constituted 'Reserve Serials' being despatched across the capital as the disorder worsens and spreads. They receive the call to go to Hackney. An elderly lady has collapsed in the street – seen, I think, by the police helicopter hovering overhead. It's all going off in the surrounding area and she clearly needs urgent help.

Police carriers are usually lively places, full of banter and silliness. This one is silent, eyes fixed straight ahead. The instruction passes from the inspector to the driver: 'Whatever you do, don't stop moving.'

Courage is feeling afraid but doing your duty all the same.
• The old lady's son has gone out into the street to assist her, but has been hit on the head by a missile thrown from who knows where. Two members of the public down. The carrier gets through and the officers jump out to form a protective shield around the injured. Somehow, they all make it out without any further injury. Mother and son will survive. At last, everyone can take a breath, and maybe call home.

I later have the honour of presenting each of the officers involved with a Commendation in recognition of their bravery.

*

It's not long after the violence has ended and I'm sitting in a community meeting in north London. The leader of the council is alongside me. We're both there to listen to the perfectly well-founded and very reasonable concerns of local people, to answer their questions and, I hope, to provide some reassurance.

I'm responding to comments from the floor when a man standing right at the back of the room shouts out suddenly, 'I hate you. Everybody hates you.' He's pretty loud and leaves no one in any doubt with regard to his opinion. I don't think we've met before, so I reassure myself that his views aren't personal. And anyway, I tell him, my wife still seemed to like me when I left home this morning, so it can't possibly be everybody. My attempts to lighten the moment aside, he clearly had an opinion about the establishment and about the police in particular. Funny how some people can't see beyond the uniform.

That said, a week or two later, I find myself in another community meeting, this time with a group made up primarily of local church leaders. I tell them the story of the shouting man and, in response, one of the vicars calls out, 'I love you. Everybody loves you.' Which is kind of him.

*

So what were the riots all about? Any number of possibilities of course. An overwhelming expression of collective fury? A vivid display of widespread disaffection and frustration? A form of legitimate protest gone badly wrong? An outpouring of anti-authoritarian sentiment? A lawless orgy of violence and materialism? An unmissable opportunity to smash things up and throw bricks at the feds? A self-defeating madness, doing far more harm than good to the communities affected?

Everyone will have their opinion. For me, there's a bit of all of the above. That said, for those rampaging through JD Sports and the Vodafone shop, loading up on the latest trainers and mobiles, it would be difficult to argue any kind of noble cause. Whatever it was about, though, it certainly represented some kind of a watershed.

*

It's several months later and I've been invited to address the congregation at St George's Church in Holborn. It's just round the corner from the station and John, the parish priest, has volunteered as a chaplain for the local Old Bill. As I'm speaking, I make a simple request of the congregation. 'The next time you see a police officer walking down the street, go up and thank them for what they do.' I explain that, on the whole, people just don't tend to do that sort of thing. I tell them it will be worth it just to see the expression on the officer's face.

The following week, I'm in full uniform, walking from the office to a meeting at the town hall. I hear someone call out to me and turn to see an elderly lady making her way slowly towards me. I recognise her from the Sunday service, but she hasn't made the connection. 'Officer,' she says, 'I just want to thank you for the amazing job that you and your colleagues do.' I grin and thank her. It's the best thing that's happened to me all week.

And it makes me think. There are times as a police officer when I just want to bury my head in my hands: Stephen Lawrence, Plebgate, Hillsborough – the list goes on. The sins of the past and the sins of the present, conspiring and causing even good people to doubt us. There can be no escaping the fact that we have, to a very significant extent, brought it on ourselves. Society has every right to expect higher standards of police officers than they do of anyone else. That is because of the promise each of us made and the powers each of us has been given. Where we betray that promise or abuse those powers, it is absolutely right that we are held to account.

I am more painfully aware than anyone I know of some of the faults and failings of the police service in this country. I have seen them at first hand and there are no excuses. But – and this is important – I am also more passionately aware than anyone I know of the remarkable brilliance of the police service and the vast majority of its people. When you stop to think about what it is that we're here to do, you are presented with an entirely extraordinary set of duties and responsibilities: the job is to save lives; to find the lost; to protect the vulnerable; to confront the violent; to pursue the dangerous; to comfort the mourning; to seek justice on behalf of those no longer able to seek it for themselves; to step into harm's way; sometimes to risk it all.

While accepting that we can fall short of such ideals, it remains a remarkable list. This is what we, quite rightly, ask and expect of our police. And I for one wouldn't have it any other way.

I suspect that we've all had the experience of passing a

police cordon, at the scene of a crime or a car crash, and wondering what was going on. I have the honour of working alongside those who operate on the other side of the blue-and-white tape. They tread where most would fear to go and, invariably, they do so with a mixture of compassion, courage and grace.

A former Met Commissioner used a wonderful phrase to describe what that means in practice. He spoke of the 'everyday heroism' of those who police our streets. I've never heard it put better.

So what's my point? Simply that there is a need to redress the imbalance evident in so much of the contemporary public narrative about policing. That is in no way an attempt to divert attention from some of our very evident failings, but rather to seek a broader perspective.

Every now and then, when I stop to listen to what's being said about policing in this country, it can start to sound a little like a variation on that tired old football chant: 'You're shit and you know you are . . .' For some, it's an accusation, for others a product of experience and for still others it's a taunt. In many instances, it's just a lazy repetition of the noise of the crowd. And the story becomes: the police are racist, the police are corrupt, the police are untrustworthy, the police are inept.

Well, sometimes we are and some of us can be. Some of our failings have been catastrophic and some of the consequences unthinkable. Sometimes it's an individual officer at fault, sometimes it's the whole institution. And, either way, the responsibility for putting things right is ours and ours alone. But it's not the whole story. It's not even most of the story. There is more to be said. There's no other job, in Britain at least, that comes close to this one in terms of the level of threat faced by frontline staff. Every single day, there are dozens of assaults on police officers in England and Wales, several thousand attacks every year. And each of us is an explicit terrorist target.

There's no other job that comes close in terms of the trauma that frontline staff are exposed to: murder scenes and cot deaths, fatal crashes and extremist executions, child abuse and domestic violence, decaying corpses and the debris of shattered lives.

There's no other job that comes close in terms of the unique context in which police officers operate: at the margins of society, in the face of hostility and conflict, in between life and death, in defence of those who don't want us, but still need us, in among the gangs and the troubled homes, in the streets where extreme poverty is a neighbour to extraordinary wealth.

There's no other job that comes close in terms of the operational complexity that police officers are faced with: neighbourhoods with something like 200 mother-tongue languages spoken, demographic movement and change on an extraordinary scale, in a shrinking world where global events have immediate local impacts, technological change at a headlong pace and the endlessly shifting patterns of crime that follow. All in an age of austerity, with savings required on a scale without precedent.

There's no other job that comes close in terms of the

scrutiny that police officers are subject to: from politicians, from the media, from the Independent Police Complaints Commission, from the public we come into contact with and from anyone with an armchair and an opinion.

It is absolutely right that we should be held to that higher standard. But the relentless hostility and uninformed agendas that characterise so much of the public conversation about us can sometimes take my breath away. In the vast majority of cases, the vast majority of the time, my experience of policing – and of the people who do this job – bears little or no comparison with the sound coming from the terraces. In fact, the best of them are the best that people can be. They are brave and they are brilliant. They are capable and they are compassionate. They are fearless and they are funny. They are patient and they are professional. They are long-suffering and they are loyal. They are humble and they are humane. They are the everyday heroes and heroines who police our streets.

XIV. *The Siege of London*

It's late April 2012 and it's a bright, peaceful afternoon in London's West End. Sitting in my office, high up in Holborn Police Station, I take in a view of the City dominated by the domes of the Old Bailey and St Paul's in the foreground. Justice and mercy, side by side.

Suddenly and without any prior warning, multiple calls start coming through on the radio, initially to a suspected fire in an office block on Tottenham Court Road; then to possible hostages taken by an armed suspect at the same location. Whatever bit of paperwork I was doing doesn't matter any more. I just drop everything and go, grabbing my body armour and kit belt on the way.

Down thirteen floors, frustrated by the too-slow lift, running along corridors and scrambling down the last set of stairs to the Back Yard. I climb into the front passenger seat of an available IRV as Naomi, my Staff Officer, takes the wheel. I try to listen to the radio as Naomi picks her way expertly and swiftly through the slow traffic. Smatterings of incomplete detail are coming through from officers arriving at the scene, but no one can offer anything resembling a complete picture. All we do know is that we appear to have a genuine hostage situation. My thoughts are moving faster than the car as I try to work out what's happening, as I try to come up with the beginnings of a plan.

The Duty Officer arrives at the scene ahead of me and calls up to say that he's going to enter the building. I tell him to hold off. He needs to be one step back, directing the troops, not diving in. I understand the instinct, but I also understand the need to keep a clear head. And, in any case, we have no idea what kind of threat we're facing. If this is what we think it is, the last thing we need is a police officer being added to the numbers of those being held or, worse still, being killed or seriously injured.

As we pull up just short of the scene – a nondescript office building on the east side of the road – the area is already at a complete standstill: buses pulled over to one side, cars and taxis stacking up and emergency services vehicles beginning to accumulate. What the hell is going on?

The *Daily Telegraph* front page of the following day will call it 'The Siege of London'.

Piece by piece, more information begins to come through. The suspect is a middle-aged white male, dressed in a suicide vest – wired and ready to go – and carrying a flame-thrower. Multiple hostages are believed to have been taken at the location, their condition unknown.

As I'm trying to take it all in – the sheer damn seriousness of it all – I hear the sound of windows shattering several floors above me. I look up as computers and office equipment start to rain down on the street, a steady cascade of glass and hardware.

There's an immediate stampede of insistent questions competing for attention. Who is our suspect? Get the cordons in place, and get the distances right. How many hostages have we got? Who are they? What state are they in? We're going to need more officers – a lot more officers. Call the TSG to help us with evacuations. Where are the PCs who arrived first on scene? Is everyone accounted for? It is just a matter of weeks before the London Olympic Games – are we dealing with a full-blown terrorist attack?

All around me, people get stuck in: cordon tape, radio traffic, shouted instructions from multiple directions, buzzing phones, new teams arriving and deploying, fresh briefings, hardware. That sense of movement, of urgency, of speed being of the essence. Everyone knows something; no one knows everything. We are making critical choices and decisions in fractions of seconds, based on limited information and imperfect knowledge, the consequences of which will stay with us for ever. And I'm there in the middle of it all: thinking; praying; talking; listening; trusting; juggling; hoping; wondering...

Establish a command structure. What kind of weapons has the suspect got and how many? Is he operating alone? Call for Traffic Officers to help with road closures. Anyone injured? Get the DCI on the phone to establish an Intelligence Cell. We're going to need a team of hostage negotiators – get them running now. Specialist firearms officers too. All of this is happening in moments. Naomi is standing next to me, trying to write it all down. Find somewhere to base the command team. The local Starbucks is as good as anywhere. Clear the customers out and set up in there. Can somebody brief the fire-brigade and ambulance crews with what we know and make sure they are standing by?

This is now a Major Incident – something significant involving all three 999 services – and I'm in charge. But there's no opportunity to pause and feel the weight of responsibility. There's a job to be done. Pressure and intensity and adrenalin and strain. People's lives in our hands. The security and resilience of one of the world's great cities being tested.

The bomb disposal team are on the way – don't broadcast their arrival over the radio. Anything on the hostages, for crying out loud? Call the late turn in early; this could be a long one.

We're now in the process of shutting down what feels like half of central London. I've got two different bosses on the phone, both wanting to know what's happening. One is the on-call Commander for Major Incidents, the other is the head of the firearms teams. They both mean well but, to be honest, I could do with a moment or two to think straight. What I really need them to do is send me every available resource in the Met and then give me room to breathe and space to do my job.

I assemble all the team leaders in our makeshift command post: the Duty Officer and other local supervisors, the Trojan and TSG inspectors, the fire-brigade and ambulance leads. The numbers swell as other units arrive: negotiators, firearms, traffic and the rest. I tell them what little we know. And then I listen to the advice and recommendations of a group of specialists who are brilliant at what they do. Remarkable people, one and all. I trust them.

*

No let-up in the pace. Not for one moment. What's the plan? It's not complicated. Contain and negotiate, save life, and get everyone out of here safely – suspect included. Everything else can wait.

Are all the cordons in yet? What am I missing? Any update on the hostages? Numbers? Injuries?

The Commissioner's office is on the phone. 'I know you're busy, but . . .' Actually, I am a bit busy. Would you mind ringing back later on?

Do we have the Emergency Action plan agreed yet – contingencies if we need to get into the building in a hurry? What about some holding lines for the press? Because, within a very short space of time, the whole thing is live on the rolling news channels. And the watching world is about to start speculating on what's happening and what we're doing about it. It seems to me that talking about policing from the comfort of a broadcaster's studio is marginally more straightforward than doing it for real.

*

We get our first break. Someone has offered up a possible name for our suspect. It appears that he may be a former client of the company whose computers are now littering the street. Evidently not a happy customer.

We begin to run checks and the possibility comes back

that he's ex-military – a former Royal Engineer. A soldier, in possession of explosives and other weapons, with hostages. In Tottenham Court Road in the middle of the afternoon.

I will never forget the response of the man from the Bomb Squad, now standing next to me, to this latest piece of news.

'If he's ex-REME, he knows how to take that whole building down.'

This has just gone to a whole new level. Extend the cordons – we're far too close. We move our operational base from Starbucks to a department store further up the road. Are the negotiators ready to go? Are the specialist firearms teams in position?

For just a handful of moments, time slows and, once again, Markham Square fills my thoughts. The only difference is that there I just had to concentrate on doing my job as a negotiator. Here, I'm responsible for everything. There are so many things that could go wrong. Please, God, don't let it end badly.

*

The waiting game. Everyone is briefed. Everyone understands the plan and knows their part in it. The negotiators put the first call in, as snipers somewhere up above us survey the scene through telescopic sights. Hold your nerve, everyone.

*

Eventually, I am given the news that the hostages are out – we think all of them. All of them are unharmed. We need to look after them, but we also need to debrief them urgently. Our suspect is still in there and we want as much information as possible about him: his appearance, his demeanour, his motivations, his intentions. And we want details about the scene, from layout, entry and exit points to obstacles and anything else we might be able to make use of.

They tell us that the flame-thrower works and that the vest looks real enough. And the words of the man from the Bomb Squad are playing on my mind.

Our plans and our people are all in place. Several Tube stations are closed and the buses are all on diversion. Everyone – every last member of the team – is doing a blindingly good job. The on-call Commander arrives to handle the press, which gives me one less thing to think about. We're still live on the twenty-four-hour news feeds and our every move will be analysed, picked apart and second-guessed. As Theodore Roosevelt said, 'It is not the critic who counts.'

How much is this costing the local economy in terms of lost business? Hundreds of thousands, I expect. And goodness only knows how many coppers, firefighters and paramedics we've got here now.

One of the Deputy Assistant Commissioners is on the phone – Steve Kavanagh. He's a good friend and, refreshingly, he's not actually asking me for anything. He's checking that I'm all right and asking whether I need anything. I appreciate the call. And it seems that the telly in his office is giving a better view of unfolding events than I have on the ground. I hope my family know I'm OK.

*

Then it ends, almost as swiftly as it began. The negotiators have been talking to the suspect and doing their job well.

Our man has said that he's ready to come out and we actually have to slow things down to make sure we're ready for him.

The instructions are passed along. He must be stripped to the waist, with his hands empty and above his head. We still have no idea what he might be capable of and, quite rightly, no one is taking any chances. He emerges into the street, bare-chested and handcuffed.

And I exhale.

He's not ex-military after all. It turns out the company has two clients with exactly the same name. What are the chances of that? And, while the flame-thrower is viable, the suicide vest will turn out to be a fake. Not that anyone knows that yet.

It could have ended in any number of ways. But it ended well, with not a scratch on anyone, including him. Had it been otherwise, I daresay you would have heard a whole lot more about it.

The tension falls away and I begin a round of handshakes and heartfelt thank yous. I'm tired. I wander from the department store out onto Tottenham Court Road, where I take in a panorama that might have been pulled straight from a film set: deserted pavements, abandoned vehicles, debris everywhere, lengths of blue-and-white tape fluttering in the breeze. I hand the scene over to the DCI and his team of investigators and catch a lift back to the station.

*

Today, in the heart of the capital, I have witnessed the brilliant best of the Met in full flow: PCs on cordons, support officers on junctions, armed officers on rooftops, the TSG standing by, detectives interviewing victims and witnesses, negotiators huddled in the back of a cramped van, firearms officers kitted up and ready, the bomb disposal team ready to go in, sergeants and inspectors marshalling everyone, all of them prepared to put themselves in harm's way. These are the days that take it out of you, when you empty yourself for the sake of the job. But these are also the days that you join for, when you stumble home with a big grin on your face, exhausted and elated – with your head spinning and that priceless sense of a job well done. These are the days when you save lives and talk people down. These are the days when you become the front-page news for all the right reasons. These are the days when you could not possibly feel prouder to be a police officer.

*

The suspect will later plead guilty to false imprisonment, criminal damage and being responsible for a bomb hoax. He will be sentenced to six years in prison.

XV. *Falling Down*

Towards the end of 2012, two years into my time at Camden, I get called up to the Yard to see another of the Deputy Assistant Commissioners – the man in charge of policing all thirty-two London boroughs. My first instinct is that I must have done something wrong or, perhaps, that one of my teams has done something wrong. My presumptions are a sign of the times: there's a new senior management regime in place, performance pressures are intensifying, budgets are tightening, operational challenges are mounting. Everyone is under scrutiny (not all of it supportive) and everyone is under pressure. One or two of my colleagues in other boroughs have experienced a particular kind of discomfort associated with critical scrutiny from on high and the rest of us are on our toes. It's not the easiest or the most enjoyable of environments to be working in.

But, on this occasion, I'm mistaken. The DAC, a man I get on well with, sits me down in his office and gets straight to the point. He tells me that he wants me to take over the

Borough Command at Southwark. His request catches me unawares, but the fact that I'm being offered the post seems to represent something of a professional compliment. Southwark is one of the Met's really big beasts – one of four or five boroughs recognised as being particularly challenging to police, primarily because of the sheer volume of serious crime that is committed there. Camden is no small undertaking, but Southwark is a step up in terms of operational complexity and professional intensity.

I have no plans to leave north London. I love the current job and we just seem to be getting somewhere, but it is a compelling proposition. And, somewhere at the back of my mind is the thought that the offer on the table may not be one I can refuse. So I say yes.

*

On the Sunday afternoon before I'm due to start, Bear and the girls help me load up the boot of the car with all my stuff. We head over to Southwark Police Station and through the door to my new office. It's a different sort of family outing, but it matters to me that they are able to take part in the adventure.

The girls clamber onto chairs and sit round the small meeting table, equipped with an assortment of paper and pens. As I unpack boxes and sort myself out, they create assorted works of art to decorate the place with, accompanied by handwritten messages of encouragement for their dad. I arrange photos of them all on my desk and put a large poster of my favourite film, *The Shawshank Redemption*, up on the wall. I love the line printed across the top of it: *Fear can hold you prisoner; hope can set you free.*

*

On my second morning in the new job, before my feet have really touched the ground, the phone rings. It's a call from Camden: one of those you're not expecting; one of those you hope never to receive. Last night, one of my former officers died on duty.

Adele was chasing a robbery suspect through the back streets of Kentish Town, doing a job she loved and was very good at, when she simply fell to the ground. Seems she had a massive heart attack. She was just thirty years old and, though I didn't know her well, I knew her well enough. She was one of the best of us.

Andy and Lucy – two of her close friends and some of my favourite people – were on duty with her when it happened. They were with her at the end. Andy calls me with the news. It's utterly heart-breaking.

*

And there will be no rest. The demands of my new job are going to be relentless. I did a bit of homework before heading south of the river and have a reasonable idea of what the most urgent policing concerns are going to be. It all comes down to three separate – though related – types of crime: knife offences, street robbery and serious violence involving young people. All are showing long-term upward trends in the borough and, taken together, present a picture of Southwark that is by far the most challenging in London. We have the highest levels of reported serious youth violence, by far the highest volume of reported knife crime and the second-highest number of reported robberies (though with comfortably the highest proportion where the suspect is armed with a blade). It is unbelievably serious stuff. The stuff of life and death.

*

Within a handful of weeks of arriving, I'm faced with the fearfully familiar. Dogan Ismail is murdered. He was seventeen years old and he died from a single stab wound to the heart, following some sort of dispute over nothing more than a mobile phone.

A forensic tent covers his body at the scene of the crime. Just a couple of feet away, bunches of flowers have been placed against a wall. Only, they aren't for Dogan. It's too soon for him. The bouquets are for another young man, murdered about three months before in almost exactly the same spot.

The hunt for Dogan's killer leads to the arrest and subsequent conviction of a fifteen-year-old boy. A fifteen-year-old boy, guilty of murdering a seventeen-year-old boy. A child killing a child.

The murder happened on the Aylesbury Estate. It's a couple of miles from where we live and, if you've heard the name, it's almost certainly for the wrong reasons. It's the place where, in 1997, Tony Blair chose to give his first public speech as a newly elected Prime Minister. The choice of venue and the accompanying symbolism of deep urban malaise were deliberate.

The Aylesbury is vast: 2,700 flats and houses, designed to accommodate somewhere in the region of 10,000 people. Stretching north from Burgess Park along the full length of the Albany Road, you could spend plenty of time getting lost in there. Even before Dogan's murder, it had my attention.

The local residents and community leaders I meet are wonderful – personalities at odds with the recurring media portrayal of their neighbourhood. But then there's the place itself: relentless grey buildings characterised by an indeterminate sadness, warrens of walkways and endless dark corners, unwelcoming stairwells and precious little green space. Hindsight can make the foolish wise but, really, what were the architects and planners thinking? The design of the place was a disaster from the very beginning.

∗

I'm making my way along the raised walkway where Dogan was murdered, accompanied by a BBC journalist. We're wearing microphones and the cameraman at the far end is picking up everything we say. It's a couple of days since the killing and the Aylesbury stereotypes have been given free rein.

The journalist is asking me if the police have lost control of the area. I understand the reasons for the rather provocative question, but I'm not sure it's the right one to ask. The Aylesbury's story is infinitely more complicated than any basic requirement for additional enforcement, as are the lives of those who choose to resolve their disputes at the point of a knife. I'm not seeking to duck my professional responsibilities – not for one moment. The police will always be first in line in the response to violent crime. But we're only first in the line – we're the emergency response. There's so much more required in places like the Aylesbury than the sticking plasters we carry.

I feel deeply for Dogan's family, living their own private hell. And I feel deeply for the many, many good people of the estate, obliged to live with both the reality and the stigma. The news crews will come and go. Politicians too. Local folk will remain, and keep on going.

*

Just along from the murder scene, there's a large sign up on the wall of one of the blocks. It says simply, 'Nobody is not loved'. It is a statement of defiance and of rare truth. Even in the places of despair, it seems, there's grace to be found.

*

But what on earth are we going to do to stop teenagers killing one another? I know that Stop & Search isn't the long-term solution to anything. But experience has taught me that it does save lives. It's a means to an end – a way to stem the flow. It is our primary tactic.

We launch Operation Trinity on 1 January 2013 and it will run for the best part of twelve months. There's nothing remotely sophisticated about it. It isn't an attempt to solve underlying problems – it's a short-term fix, designed simply to stop the madness. In the three or four years before Trinity, the number of searches carried out by the police in Southwark had fallen dramatically. Some of that was with good reason, not least an end to the use of certain counter-terrorism search powers. But that was far from being the whole picture and it's difficult to avoid the conclusion that people are now carrying weapons on our streets, confident that they aren't going to be stopped by the police. And if not us, then who? Who is going to challenge the young men of violence? And what exactly is it that those who advocate an end to the use of Stop & Search are suggesting as an alternative?

There are endless, deeply unhelpful misconceptions about Stop & Search. Take for example the belief held by some that if the police don't find anything during an encounter on the street, the officer concerned must have done something wrong. A negative search is somehow portrayed as a negative thing. This is complete nonsense. Done well, irrespective of whether or not anything is recovered, the use of the tactic sends a clear and powerful message that the police are committed to keeping a community safe – and the conversation on the street provides an invaluable opportunity to listen and to talk, to show people that we're human after all.

A few months earlier, just as Remembrance Sunday was approaching, I'd gone out on patrol with one of the local PCs. I wanted to get to know the ground and to hear a bit about what the place was really like from someone who was actually doing the job. We put in a drugs stop on a young lad out on the street late at night. The search was negative, but he noticed the small red poppy pin I was wearing on my tie and asked me about it. I'm always happy to talk and I explained what it represented – why I was wearing it. He seemed to like it, so I took it off and gave it to him. And he smiled as he accepted it. Maybe, just maybe, he went and told some of his mates that the Old Bill aren't all bad.

And so, along with a broad range of other tactics, we

set out to increase significantly our Stop & Search activity. Understanding that this might be controversial for some, we do a lot of work in the background. I brief a number of the borough's key community organisations: the Independent Advisory Group, the Police Consultative Group and the Stop & Search Monitoring Group. I want them to understand our intentions and motivations and I want them to be able to challenge and ask questions. My experience has always been that we make better decisions when we are listening to critical friends. We brief the local press and speak at length with our local partners in Southwark council and beyond and we lay on additional training for our frontline staff. My simple message for the officers is that I want them out there saving lives.

And it works - at least to the limited extent that a short-term enforcement operation ever does. I don't tend to rely much on numbers - lies, damned lies and all that - but just occasionally they're worth reading.

During 2013, the use of Stop & Search in Southwark increases by more than 25 per cent (compared with the previous year). At the same time, reported robbery falls by more than 10 per cent, reported knife crime falls by more than 17 per cent and reported serious youth violence falls by more than 26 per cent. It doesn't require an almighty leap of faith to make some sort of connection. Interestingly, over the same period of time, the number of public complaints relating to Stop & Search falls from 40 to 29.

We draw some sort of a line and there are no more fatal stabbings during the rest of my time at Southwark.

*

My PA tells me that I'm a calming influence on the place. Well, I try to be. We're surrounded by a level of organisational pressure and operational demand the like of which I've not encountered before and my response has been to soak up as much of it as I can, without passing it on to my team. My approach is partly instinctive and partly by choice. I want people to be able to focus fully on the things that really matter (like Operation Trinity), without being distracted unnecessarily by the things that don't (like the endless performance targets that mean little and achieve nothing).

It's an approach that I hope has benefits both for my colleagues and for the borough but, though I don't recognise or understand what's happening, it is beginning to take its toll on me. I'm tired. I work long hours. I attend endless meetings at the station, at the town hall, in local community venues and anywhere else I think I might be able to do some good. I visit the midnight prayer meeting at the Nigerian church at the bottom of Lordship Lane. Whatever it takes to build bridges. I get out on patrol when I can. I spend as much time as possible with frontline officers and support staff, encouraging honest conversations, exhorting them to get out there and make a difference and thanking them for every extraordinary thing they do. Stepping back or slowing down doesn't even occur to me. There is just too much to be done. But I am running on fumes.

*

Back in the office and reports come through of a fourteen-year-old boy alleging that he's been raped.

The account given by the victim goes something like this. He was walking down the street when a male suspect approached him and produced a knife. He demanded the victim's mobile phone – but the victim didn't have one. And the suspect led him off the street and into a nearby estate. He took him up some stairs and, in the vicinity of one of the open landings, raped him. Apparently it happened in a public place, in the middle of the day.

The description given of the suspect is really specific, down to the lanyard he was wearing around his neck. The details are so vivid and so utterly unusual that I find myself wondering whether the victim has somehow imagined it all. Some of my highly experienced colleagues are asking the same question. But, within about forty-eight hours, the answer is unequivocal. Clear forensic evidence has been recovered, and a suspect has been identified. He's fifteen years old. A fifteen-year-old boy accused of raping a fourteen-year-old boy. A child accused of raping a child. Bloody hell.

Of course, the rape of a boy is no more or less shocking than the rape of a girl. Short of homicide, both are just about as brutal and dreadful as a crime can be. But something about this particular case gets through an unseen gap in my professional armour. It troubles me. Perhaps it's the ages of those involved – children who could be my sons. Maybe it's the fact that it happened in broad daylight in a residential community. Or it might just be that I've hit some sort of tipping point, the accumulation of endless dark tales told over the course of a policing lifetime.

The thing is, not many people phone the police to say that they're having a good day. Instead, they call to say:

'My boy's been shot.'

'My girlfriend's missing.'

'It's dark and I'm being followed.'

'The house next door is on fire.'

'My ex-boyfriend is trying to smash down my front door.'

'There's a car on its roof in the middle lane.'

'I've just been spat at in the street.'

'My husband was out drinking last night and now I can't wake him.'

'My house has been broken into and everything that matters to me has been taken.'

'I've just seen a cyclist knocked down by a bus.'

'It's all kicking off in the pub next door.'

'I haven't seen my neighbour for a week and now there are flies all over their window.'

'I can't take it any more.'

The painful privilege of policing is to be the first in line when those calls are made and the first on scene in response. I wouldn't change it for anything, but it comes at a cost. I have worked with PCs who have been shot in the line of duty. I have worked with colleagues of all ranks and grades who have ventured into the midst of unimaginable horrors. I have worked with people who have made innumerable personal sacrifices for the sake of the job. I have seen and experienced things myself that I wouldn't wish on anyone, friend or foe. I don't say any of these things to impress or alarm. I say them simply because they are true. As a society, I don't think we have even begun to understand the compound impact on police officers of repeated exposure to extreme trauma.

*

For now, I just keep on going.

We've just finished the morning briefing, a review of crimes and incidents in the last twenty-four hours and a look ahead to the day to come, and I now have the honour of presenting an Assistant Commissioner's Commendation to one of my PCs. Once the formalities are over, I ask him to tell me the full story. I'm still relatively new to the borough and it's not one I've heard before.

He tells me that he and a female colleague had been sent to a disturbance in someone's home. It's the sort of fairly routine call that comes in dozens of times a week and, invariably, doesn't amount to much. The two of them made their way into the address to deal with whatever was there. But, following their arrival, the male occupant quickly turned violent. Astonishingly so. He punched the male PC so hard in the face that he badly broke his jaw and knocked him out cold. As the officer came to, in goodness knows how much pain, the suspect was attacking his colleague and it wasn't looking good. But with no thought for his own safety, or the severe injuries he'd already sustained, he hurled himself at the assailant. Somehow the two officers managed to hold out until help got to them.

And now, my handshake and very genuine appreciation – together with a nicely framed certificate – seem a wholly inadequate response to his extraordinary bravery.

*

Away from the action, I'm dealing with the likely closure of one of the local police stations, alongside the full range of the broader and far-reaching consequences of the economic situation we find ourselves in. It's a set of circumstances being replicated throughout the capital. And there's a real strength of feeling about the anticipated loss of local community facilities, particularly among residents and politicians who want to preserve them. I hope I'm able to demonstrate that I have some understanding of their perspectives – but, both operationally and financially, I'm faced with an absence of alternatives.

The station in question is the least used by the public of all those in the borough. It's a disproportionate drain on finances and I can no longer afford to take operational officers away from their frontline duties to staff it. Actually, the decision for me is a pretty straightforward one. But those local people who feel strongly about the issue are looking for alternatives – particularly the politicians who see it, rightly or wrongly, as a potential vote winner.

Various scenarios are put to me, including the suggestion of a smaller, alternative base for police officers, at an initial cost to the public purse of a six-figure sum. I try to explain that the operational demand isn't there to justify it, that I won't be able to locate officers there and that it will be little used as a consequence. I try to explain that I'm seeking to avoid the unnecessary expenditure of one hundred thousand pounds. 'But Officer,' says a local politician to me in half-whispered, almost conspiratorial tones, 'it isn't your hundred thousand pounds.'

Well, it isn't his either, but that particular irony seems entirely lost on him. And he's quite prepared to spend it, irrespective of the fact that I'm telling him we neither want nor will be able to use the facility being suggested. To say nothing of the fact that we probably won't be able to run it once the initial funds have dried up. It's a heck of a lot of money and, off the top of my head, I could give him a dozen or more suggestions about how it might be better spent. But he's not interested.

All the while, the broader financial context is becoming ever more challenging. There's no denying the reality – the need to make savings on an unprecedented scale – but I'm bothered by the likely consequences. Policing operates in the places of greatest vulnerability and need in society – in among the broken homes and broken bones, the broken hearts and broken lives.

This is the stuff of real life and I ask myself what the cost of austerity is going to be. For the young woman trapped in an abusive relationship, caught between the horrors of staying and the terrors of going? For the child of that young woman, witnessing extreme violence on a daily basis and suffering unimaginable trauma as a consequence? For the fifteen-year-old caught on the periphery of a gang and wanting desperately to put the knife down and get the hell out? For the man in his twenties experiencing psychotic thoughts, afraid that he's going to go out and harm somebody? For the amateur shoplifter, too ashamed to ask for help at a food-bank and running out of options to feed his family? For the young woman unable to access housing or employment, now standing on the parapet and threatening to jump? For the abused child or the trafficked teenager? For the drug addict or the alcoholic, committing crime to feed a habit they just can't seem to break? For the inhabitant of an online world, subjected to bullying, threats and wickedness of every kind?

It seems to me that the cost of austerity will be greatest for those least able to bear it.

And what of the consequences for the police service itself? The fact is that policing is being challenged as never before: greater threat, greater public expectation, greater complexity, greater risk, greater scrutiny. We can't keep demanding more for less indefinitely – there has to be a breaking point. That isn't an argument against policing reform (goodness knows we need it), but it is a statement of fact.

Looking around me, I see more good coppers working under significantly greater strain than at any previous point in my career. I am too. And, at forty-something years of age, twenty-something years into my policing life, I break.

*

I am back in my office at the end of April 2013, just after news of the jumper on the bridge. I am sitting alone with the door closed, disoriented, bewildered and utterly lost. I am a blind man in a dark basement, looking for a shadow that isn't there. What on God's earth is happening to me?

*

I started to feel unwell a few weeks beforehand, on my forty-third birthday, Sunday 3 March 2013. I was visiting friends in America, taking a break from the usual routine and the relentless pressures of the day job, savouring some time and space to think and breathe.

In the evening, I attended a service at their church. And that's when it began. I was standing somewhere near the front, there was music playing and I felt something snap in the back of my head. There was no warning sign, no prior indication. It just happened. And it was absolutely a physical sensation – like an elastic band, long held at breaking point and suddenly let go. Ping.

In an instant, I knew something was wrong. Really badly wrong. Imagine emptying a bottle of ink into a glass pitcher of clear water and watching as the blackness starts to billow and unfurl. As I stood there in the church, that's what began to happen in my head. In the wide-open spaces where delight and joy would usually be found, anxiety and uncertainty fed themselves into my imagination and slowly began to obscure everything else. And it started to happen outside of me too, clouding my surroundings and moving the real world ten paces distant. I was simultaneously being overwhelmed and left behind, a child mistakenly abandoned at the side of the road.

It was deeply unsettling and incredibly frightening, but what made it worse was that there was no way I could tell anyone around me what I was feeling. I had no idea what was happening to me and I certainly didn't have the language to explain it to someone else. I suppose I was in shock. And these were just the advance echoes. If I'd understood what was to come in the weeks ahead, I'm not sure I'd have had the courage to face it. Not if I'd known how bad it was going to be.

I flew back to London as planned the following day, confused and concerned and clueless. The journey was unsettled and uncomfortable but, as I got home to Bear and the girls, things seemed to lift a little and the subsequent return to work felt like a welcome distraction. For a while, as I buried myself back into being a Borough Commander, I was able to forget about the storm gathering in the micro-climate of my mind. But only for so long.

The exhaustion became relentless, hauling me backwards like some kind of science-fiction tractor beam, and with it came a new kind of malevolent anxiety. I started to wake up in the middle of the night in a state of total panic, heart racing and head overwhelmed. I had to wake Bear, just so she could hold me, just so she could tell me that everything was going to be OK. There was no clear reason to explain it – no specific troubling dreams, no one situation or set of circumstances dragging me down more than any other. But it was happening nonetheless: everything and nothing and the darkness of the night.

I have known real sadness and genuine distress in my life, but nothing like this. Nothing remotely like this. And I was struggling just to breathe. One night, as I lay alongside Bear, I started to weep. I've never minded crying, but these were different tears. I said the only thing that was in my head. 'I feel like such a failure.' It wasn't self-pity, it was the beginnings of true despair: bottomless, merciless, endless despair. As a husband, as a father, as a police officer, as a man. I felt like a total failure. And it was just the start of my falling.

Morning would come and I would do my best to shake it

off and go again. I talked to Bear about how I was feeling and I talked to a couple of friends. But I didn't speak to anyone at work – partly because I didn't understand, partly because I was supposed to be the strong one. I was supposed to be in charge. Bafflingly, it genuinely didn't occur to me to talk to a doctor, or to seek any kind of medical help.

Over the course of a few short weeks, the exhaustion intensified. And the anxiety cut deeper. And then the depression came. The depression: a thing of raw horror and blind terror. A water-boarding of the mind.

*

What the hell? I have a wonderful wife and we have three healthy, happy children. We have an amazing set of friends and, aside from the inevitable mortgage, not a penny of debt. I don't have any dark secrets or long-hidden addictions. I have always thought that I am reasonably straightforward. And I'm in charge at Southwark, for crying out loud – one of the most challenging operational postings in the country. I am, I think, reasonably competent and capable, and I love what I do. I've dealt with endless tragedy and trauma and have managed to hold on to my humanity. But now I can barely hold a thought in my head. The cracks have been appearing for a while, but I've not understood them. I've simply tried to keep going, just as I've always done.

I lurch through another evening and morning at work. Slipping. Sliding. I am the captain going down without his ship.

I do something I've never done before: I cancel my Friday afternoon appointments and just go home. I was due to spend a few hours visiting Brixton Prison, but that simple prospect is more than I can bear. I tell myself to get some rest and an early night, and tomorrow I'll be fine. Tomorrow, I'll be fine.

I go to bed just after seven. But, not much more than an hour later, I sit up, look at Bear and say, 'I think I'm going to have to go to hospital.'

I am scared. Really, really scared. As a child, I had a recurring nightmare. In it, I was pursued by a terrifying, yeti-like monster. It hunted me through woodland and hounded me into the grounds of a large, unknown country house. And I could never outrun it. My legs would be pumping and my lungs would be burning and, always, it would be gaining on me. Eventually, I would do the only thing I could think of – fall to the ground and play dead. And it would stand over me and breathe over me. That's when I would wake up, deeply unsettled by my dreams. Depression is that monster.

For hours and days and weeks and months, there will be no waking from it. It will stand over me and breathe over me and drive me into darkness.

*

Bear is wonderful and calm and endlessly kind, just as she has been throughout the last few weeks. It isn't until many months later that I will even begin to recognise the effects of all this on her and the strain it's placing on her.

For now, the girls are all fast asleep and she needs to stay with them. So I call a friend who knows I'm struggling and ask if he'll come and pick me up. But where to? I can't go to King's, which is closest. It's late on a Friday, and A&E will likely as not be heaving with Southwark officers. The same at St Thomas's. So my friend drives me in the opposite direction, to St George's in Tooting. I've packed an overnight bag. I don't know why. Perhaps I think I'm going to be admitted just like my dad before me. But, really, I don't know anything any more.

We arrive and book in and then we sit and wait for hours. Eventually, I speak to a nurse who takes me through the obligatory and deeply unsettling questionnaire about the state of my mind. I look at him with tears in my eyes and just tell him that I'm desperate. I'm treated with kindness and given something to get me through the weekend, but that's the best they can do.

Bear has booked me in to see my GP on Monday morning. He will confirm to me that I am suffering from depression. He will give me pills. And he will refer me for emergency counselling. I'm a Hostage & Crisis Negotiator. I know all about talking to people like me. I used to be good at it, but now I'm lost for words.

*

The next day, I manage to call my boss and tell him I'm going to have to take some time off. It's no longer a choice: I have got to the very end of myself.

In my mind, I allow myself a fortnight to recover. But what happens over the next few weeks is absolutely brutal. It is an agonising, slow-motion version of a Formula 1 racing car losing control at 200mph – barrel-rolling and disintegrating to a smoking standstill at the side of the track. There are parts and fragments scattered as far as you can see and then an unbearable silence.

Things get very much worse before they start to get any better. I will be off work for seven months. I will need another two years and more after that to get back any semblance of my old self. The truth is, I will never be the same again.

*

Back to that poster on my office wall. I love *The Shawshank Redemption*. I love everything about it. But what I love most of all is the seeming endlessness of hope: 'Remember Red, hope is a good thing – maybe the best of things. And no good thing ever dies.'

Apparently, it was Napoleon, of all people, who suggested that leaders should be dealers in hope. And I guess that's so much of what I've always tried to be, in life and in work. A dealer in hope. But now I seem to be faced with the end of hope. It takes me closer to the edge than I have ever been.

Depression smashes me to the ground. Then it places its full weight on my chest, tightens its grip round my throat and hisses endless despair into my soul.

*

When I was a child, time seemed to pass at a different pace on Christmas Eve compared with Christmas Day. On the 24th, the minutes crawled so slowly that I wondered whether bedtime would ever come. But the 25th was over almost before it had begun.

It's like that now, but without a shred of the joy and anticipation associated with the festive season. The brighter hours pass in a blink, the bleakest seconds last for ever. I throw myself into the arms of the next pill. The very best moment of the day is the drug-assisted drift into the oblivion of sleep. I'm out cold for a minimum of twelve hours a night. I don't want to wake up until the storm has passed. Except that I don't know if it ever will.

From the outset, I'm told that I will get better. The reassurance comes from people like my doctor, who actually know what they're talking about. But I find it impossible to believe them. I'm unable to work – even to think about work – unable to be the husband and father I want to be, unable to hold a conversation with a close friend for more than a handful of minutes, unable to consider the future. I'm unable to do much of anything at all, except curl up into a ball and hold on to the ragged edges.

Each time I think I might be starting to improve, it knocks me down again. It is absolutely savage: a suffocating, silent agony. And it doesn't show up on X-rays.

Initially, there isn't a great deal you'd notice from the outside, apart from perhaps the slowness of my movements and the confusion in my eyes. But, gradually, the beard grows as the weight falls off.

The ebb and flow of days, respite followed by onslaught that takes my breath away. I'm anxious about being depressed. I'm depressed about being anxious. And I helter-skelter down.

A small number of my best friends call and text and visit. Tom is there for me. I can manage half an hour at most, but he and others are a lifeline. They do my hoping and believing for me. Then there are my colleagues, my brothers and sisters in blue, Adrian among them. Most of them are Borough Commanders themselves and they seem to understand, perhaps better than anyone, the sort of hell I'm crawling through. They set up a visiting rota and set aside their own troubles and sorrows for me. Theirs are kindnesses that Bear and I will never forget.

But I was the last person they expected this to happen to. Or so they tell me.

For my part, I tell them that, if they were to offer me the choice between this and the amputation of both my legs, I would give up my legs – without anaesthetic – in a heartbeat. It isn't an attempt at melodrama. I mean it.

I had always regarded myself as one of life's optimists. I had made a life – and a living – out of being capable. And now I'm not. This is a crisis of everything. And I stagger on, rebounding off the ropes and into another ferocious right hand from this bastard illness.

*

For the first time in my life, aged forty-three, I'm taking anti-depressants, quietly terrified that my health is somehow going to go the way of my dad's. I'm taking diazepam as well – anything to keep me calm and help me sleep. The only time I've come across the drug before is down in the cells, given to restless alcoholics while the next drink is beyond their reach.

I feel shame. The shame of falling, of failing. The shame of letting people down, of not being strong enough, and, in my ignorance and vulnerability, I feel the shame of mental illness. Life and work have laid me bare.

Religion fails me. The rites and recitations learned over a lifetime offer nothing now: I am prayer-less and all my certainties are undone. Somehow, though, faith flickers: a single fragment of the Psalms whispers gently and remains: 'Be still and know that I am God.' Over time, it will begin to redefine who I am and what I believe.

And, through it all, Bear is the harbour wall to whom I lash my little boat. She holds firm and true.

*

One morning, a delivery arrives at the front door – a case of rather fine claret. It's from a friend who knows exactly how life can be when the lights go out. He's included a simple handwritten card that says, 'From one fruitcake to another...' I'm not drinking, so I hand the bottles over, one at a time, to the people who visit.

*

While I am grateful for the kindness of my work colleagues, I can't bear to think about the job itself. On 22 May 2013, Fusilier Lee Rigby is murdered by terrorists in Woolwich, in circumstances that defy comprehension. They appear to target him as a soldier, running him down in a car, before hacking him to death using knives and a meat cleaver.

Richard, a close friend and colleague, is the local Borough Commander. He's there. He sees it all. More than that, he's responsible for the policing response. Not long ago, had it happened on my patch, that would have been me. I'd have been in the thick of it. I'd have chosen to be there, spurred on by that sense of duty and a desire to be at the heart of a story played out on a global stage.

Now, I can't even look at the pictures, much less read the accounts of what happened there. I can't even begin to cope with the horror of it all. I've lost my nerve, I've lost my balance, I've lost my footing. I've lost myself. The phone rings and I can't bear to answer it. So I lie quietly, watching an old Ashes Test match.

For weeks on end, it's just about all I can do – lie motionless on the sitting-room floor and watch England beat Australia. I see the players running and competing and catching and celebrating, and I feel a kind of biting jealousy. I want to be able to do what they're able to do. Not to the same standard, of course, but just to be able to run, to smile, to take a tumble and get up again. All of it as far beyond me as it's possible to be. I used to run a borough; now I can just about run a bath.

This isn't sadness. Sadness is to depression as a puddle is to the Pacific.

On the days I manage to get up and out of the front door, I shuffle to the end of the road to buy a newspaper. I watch ordinary people walking past and I envy them. I want to be anyone but me.

*

Alone with my thoughts.

Give me any illness but this one. Give me cancer. It is a stupid, senseless thought of course, but one that seems perfectly reasonable at this particular moment. Cancer might take my body in excruciating fashion, but this is taking my mind. And that reality presents an entirely different order of fear and pain.

My dad has just been diagnosed with cancer. My mum and my sister Annie have both survived cancer. People understand cancer. They would rally round and support my family. They would applaud my courage and celebrate my inner strength. And I might just feel a little bit proud of myself. But this? What is there to admire here?

*

I read a book by a doctor: a wise, simple and compassionate book. He explains some of what is happening to me and I begin to understand that I'm not the only one. But he is also honest enough to admit that the more the experts learn about mental illness, the more they realise they don't know. It's not just me who is struggling to make any kind of sense of it all.

With the little strength I have, I begin the process of trying to work out what just happened to me. The reality is that I will never know for sure. The mind is a mystery and any attempt to isolate precise cause and effect involves a significant amount of guesswork. It is a collision, a complexity, a confusing combination of circumstances.

I think of the twenty years' wear and tear at, or close to, the frontline of policing: shift working, endless long hours over an extended period of time, being there when people die, being there when people mourn, being there when imagined horrors become real. It is the repeated invitation into life's dark recesses and the recurring challenge to give up on hope.

And we all have our limits. We all have our breaking points.

Perhaps I've seen too much: broken victims and horrific crime scenes, fatal accidents and burnt-out homes, the heartbroken families of those who have gone, the staggering drunks and shuffling junkies, the abandoned and the abused, the family home with faeces on the floor and no kind of love, police officers sitting, ashen-faced, trying to come to terms with the things they've had to deal with. Each time, I have absorbed a little more sadness.

And, through the arc of those years, there are days and moments in days that leave deeper scars, the deepest scars of all – some you can see, most that you can't. I think of Markham Square. I think of that seventeenth-floor window ledge in north London. I think of my first murder scene, and the ones that followed. I think of the sudden deaths, the stabbings and the shootings. I think of the punch in the face and my blood-soaked shirt. I think of Kodjo Yenga and Ben Kinsella and the other young men I never met, but whose stories will remain with me for ever. I think of the faces and the places. I remember them all.

Beyond all of that, there are the realities of my current role, some of them extraordinary, some of them excruciating. The job at Southwark is unlike any other – every kind of carnage almost every single day. I love it though. I love the people. I love the extraordinary job they do on a daily basis. I love celebrating their achievements. I love the responsibility. I love being in the arena. I love coming home at the end of the day with a tale to tell.

What I don't love is the conspiracy of the unimportant – the headlong pursuit of all the wrong things. There are the frequently meaningless meetings and the endlessly shifting performance priorities, the thin-witted pursuit of numbers at the expense of anything truly meaningful and the myopic requirements for quick fixes at the expense of real and lasting change. They make an impossible job that little bit harder to do.

As a Borough Commander – surrounded by some of the most brilliant and brave men and women you could ever hope to work with – I have found myself, on far too many occasions, trying to make a difference in spite of, rather than because of, the world around me. And that wears you down.

It's not all about work of course. There is the flat-out pace of London life – the world moving at a speed that isn't good for any of us: fast living, fast food, fast cars, fast forward, faster broadband, faster, faster, faster.

Gandhi said, 'There is more to life than increasing its speed.' But I don't think anyone was listening.

And, of course, there's a life story: the things that have nothing to do with policing, but everything to do with me. Everyone has their story.

*

I'm settled back down on the floor watching another Ashes triumph. Seeing Australia getting hammered has become a form of therapy. In the room next door, I can hear Jessie, my eldest daughter, playing the piano. I've not been able to do much as a dad in recent months, but I can still be a dad. I can still talk like a dad.

I call out to her, 'How did you get so good at playing the piano?'

She pauses her recital, and without missing a beat, calls back to me, 'How did you get so good at watching the cricket?'

I suppose that, for both of us, it's been a question of practice.

*

My middle daughter Charlie is ready for bed. I settle down alongside her to read *The Horse and His Boy*, the third of the Chronicles of Narnia. As I relive the magic and myth of my own childhood, she is spellbound. 'Onward and Upward! To Narnia and the North!' I have always loved tales of adventure and the ones I've loved most of all are those where the endings are happy and where the heroes are triumphant.

*

When I first fell ill, I much preferred to stay quietly indoors. As the weeks passed and I improved, I tried to get outside every day.

When we manage to get out of the house as a family, we head for one of the local parks: fresh air for me, a break from the four walls for Bear and room for the girls to run around in. Today, the weather is beautiful and we've driven the couple of miles to Dulwich Park. I sit on a picnic blanket in the wide-open spaces as everyone else runs and climbs and squeals. Emily, our youngest, is approaching her fifth birthday and chooses this moment to provide us with evidence of the fact that she's been paying attention at school – to the voices in the playground at least. As the sandwiches are being unwrapped, she plants herself in the middle of us all, a picture of cherubic innocence, and waits for an appropriate break in the conversation before uttering a single, simple word. It comes from nowhere: 'Fuck.'

Her sisters look horrified. Bear and I are too busy snorting into our sleeves to offer any sort of rebuke and, emboldened, she practises her pronunciation: 'Fuck... fuck... fuck...'

She has no idea what she's saying, but she seems delighted by the reaction. And it is a wonderful thing to be laughing again. There hasn't been too much of that in the last few months.

XVI. *The Long Road Back*

It's a haunting, humbling thing for a man to acknowledge that he is broken. For those first few months, I was too ill to care. My whole world narrowed to the next breath and the next pill. But, eventually, there comes a point when you are well enough to know just how ill you are.

I know that I am broken.

To make matters worse, there is the realisation that mine has not been a discreet falling. I was the man in charge when it happened and there can be no avoiding the simple fact that I am no longer there. My local MPs (an impressive selection of government ministers, past and present) know about it. The chief exec of the local authority and the council leader know about it. The Commissioner knows, of course, as do the rest of the top brass. My mates, my fellow Borough Commanders, all know. It's a daunting thing to accept that everyone knows: that there's no hiding and hoping no one will notice.

The final insult comes from a journalist, fishing for a

non-existent scoop, who thinks I must be missing from my post as a consequence of some form of wrongdoing on my part, who believes that I've been removed from my job for reasons that have been kept from public view. His nonsense never gets published.

*

The slow tick of time. The long, steep climb. Little improvements.

Friends tell me that I'm brave. If there is virtue to be found in continuing to breathe when your mind is falling and your soul is stalling, then I suppose I am not entirely without courage. But I don't feel brave. Bravery seems to me to require some element of choice – of reaching the fork in the road and selecting the narrow way – but I'm not sure that I have too many options.

Inside Shawshank Prison, Andy suggests to Red that it all comes down to a simple choice between living and dying. Well, dying appeals to me even less than living, so living is all there is. Getting better is the only thing I can do.

Bear is the brave one. She looks after me. She looks after the girls, more or less as a single parent, keeping things as steady and as normal as she can for them. She looks after our home. She holds down a full-time job, working as a teaching assistant at the girls' school. And she chooses not to trouble me with her tears.

She is as extraordinary as a human being can be and I discover a depth of love that I have never known before. *In sickness and in health.*

When we made those promises on our wedding day,

neither of us imagined it would come to this. But we find a way through it together. We work out what helps me mend – hot baths, hot chocolate, bowls of cashew nuts, not too much noise, making a point of resting when I'm feeling OK. And I learn to recognise and respond to the signs my body gives me. We use a scoring system: one to ten, physically and mentally. Whenever she needs to know how I'm doing, Bear asks me for a number.

She walks home from school at lunchtime every day and I make us something healthy to eat. We sit out in the little yard at the back of our house, talking and breathing in the sunlight. She is the only person with whom I feel completely safe. We talk about silver linings, about the unexpected good-ness to emerge from the darkness: the kindness of friends, time with the girls, time with each other, time to learn and grow. I think we were fortunate enough to have a pretty good marriage before I was ill, but we are starting to build an even stronger one now.

She asks me to shave off my beard. It's a visible reminder of my illness that she could do without. And I start to write. I begin to record my story and, as I do so, find that I can remember things in vivid detail: scenes and smells and emotions and sensations, people and places and moments in time. Writing them down offers a kind of catharsis. It seems to help the healing process.

*

After an imagined eternity (in reality it was about three months), the monster slowly begins to retreat. The drugs kick in and my mood gradually begins to lift. Pills don't work for everyone, but they seem to work for me, and I don't hesitate in taking them.

As a young adult, I had looked on helplessly and despairingly as my dear dad refused to take any form of medication for his bipolar disorder. Courses of treatment were prescribed and ignored and so, through a mixture of stubbornness and ignorance, he denied himself the respite that might just have been his all along. The remembrance of watching him makes my decision easy.

In this supposedly enlightened world of ours, there remains an undoubted stigma associated with taking antidepressants. I'm sure Dad felt it, even if he was unable to articulate it. Now that Dad has cancer, he doesn't struggle to accept the diagnosis or the need for chemotherapy. Why should the mind be any different?

My sister Annie has had her thyroid removed (cancer again) and, as a consequence, needs to take the drug thyroxin for the rest of her life. There's a chemical lacking in her body but, wonder of wonders, there's a tablet she can take to make up for the deficiency. Why should it be any different with my head? If I need to be on meds for the rest of my life, then so be it. Everyone else can just get over it.

*

While I'm following doctor's orders, I also get to know Anna, a wise and wonderful counsellor who begins, quietly and gently, to help me untangle myself. We meet every week. I do most of the talking, she does most of the listening and we take it one step at a time.

I tell her about the places I've been and the things I've

seen. And she tells me that it's OK to feel – that, actually, it's the natural, normal, human thing to do. Everyone needs someone to talk to sometimes.

In an early session, she asks me how much of my identity is found in being a police officer. It's a question that unsettles me for a while and prompts a recognition of the fact that, to a significant extent, what I do has come to define who I am. This isn't just any old job, this is The Job. And I am the Borough Commander, the Incident Commander, the Match Commander. I am the Hostage Negotiator and the dinner party conversationalist with endless tales to tell. I am the man in the arena, in the eye of the storm, inside the cordon. At least, I was. Now I am none of those things. But I am still me.

*

Despite the continuing improvements in my state of mind, a deep exhaustion remains. Physically, I'm still struggling – walking up the down escalator, wading through waist-deep mud, hauling myself through an endless snowdrift. I just have to surrender to it all and let my body mend.

For the first time in my life, I begin to discover what it really means to rest. And it's not just about the absence of activity, though that's important – it's also about the presence of peace. I rest and I rest and I rest. Be still and know...

*

I finally make it back to work in December 2013, seven months after I last walked out of the station. But I don't go back to Southwark. For as long as it had remained a possibility, I persisted with the notion that I'd return to the old job. For as long as he was able, my boss had kept the place open for me. But we were maintaining the same illusion and we both realise eventually that it isn't going to happen. Accepting the fact involves a kind of grieving, not least for the loss of invincibility and the inability to perform the feats of yesterday.

For now, all I will be able to manage is four hours a day, three days a week, based somewhere far removed from the policing frontline. I ask to be given a role working for Cressida Dick, a wonderful senior officer I trust and admire. She's the immensely capable Assistant Commissioner in charge of UK counter-terrorism and one of the kindest and most decent bosses I know. She made time in her ridiculously busy work schedule to come and visit me when I was still off and she knows and understands my limits. I don't have it within me to chase terrorists, but there are plenty of less dramatic, but no less engaging things I will be able to do for her behind the scenes, in my own time and without any of the old pressures.

I travel on the Tube for the first time in a long time. I stand still on the escalators, finished and done with the flat-out pace of before. I exit at St James's Park and make my way through security at Scotland Yard. I haven't done that in a while, but it feels OK. I always wanted to get back, I just didn't know whether I'd be able to.

It will be another nine months before I'm back to working full hours and, even then, I will be operating at a fraction of the capacity I had before. I genuinely have no idea how I managed to do the job I used to do.

As I consider what might come next, I find myself thinking increasingly about the things that have to matter more. Years ago, I discovered an extraordinary little book written by Martin Luther King. It was called *The Measure of a Man* (though it might equally have been called *The Measure of a Woman*). I lent it to a friend and never got it back. Having discovered that it's back in print, I manage finally to get my hands on a new copy and it makes just as much of an impression second time round as it did the first.

The content is simple (a large part of its appeal while I'm still struggling to concentrate for any length of time), setting out what Dr King describes as the three dimensions of life: length, breadth and height.

> The length of life as we shall think of it here is not its duration or its longevity, but it is the push of life forward to achieve its personal ends and ambitions. It is the inward concern for one's own welfare.

My own welfare. I'm not sure it's something I'd given too much thought to before I fell.

At the age of five, I had believed that it was my job to look after Mum while Annie was fighting her first cancer battle. No one had told me otherwise. At the age of seventeen and for many years afterwards, I had understood that it was my role to look after my family in the absence of Dad. At the age of twenty-two, I had taken the Oath and, for the next two decades and more, had known that it was my duty to look after the people of London. Now I'm a dad myself and I have three of the most beautiful girls in the world to look after. I don't regret any of those things.

> Every individual has a responsibility to be concerned about himself enough to consider what he is made for. After he discovers his calling, he should set out to do it with all the strength and power in his being ...

That's what I've tried to do with my life and with my policing life in particular. It's still what I want to do. But it turns out that, in order to be able to do so, I actually need to look after myself – to retain that inward concern for my own well-being.

Recovery isn't linear, a simple straight line between then and now. There are any number of jarring moments and sudden changes of direction, some of them incredibly painful. But I am getting better.

The breadth of life is about the world and, more specifically, the people around me. It is about community and neighbourliness; about a genuine concern for one another.

> An individual has not started to live until he can rise above the narrow confines of his individualistic concerns to the broader concerns of all humanity ...

> May it not be that the problem with the world today is that individuals as well as nations have been overly concerned with the length of life, devoid of the breadth ... ?

And it is in the breadth of life that I discover so much of my healing. It begins with Bear and her unconditional, unhesitating love for me. Getting married to a no-nonsense North Yorkshire farmer's daughter with a great big heart turns out to have been one of the better decisions I've made in my life. I learn to share the journey and the load with her and to listen whenever she has something to suggest or say. She's usually right about things.

Then there are the girls, not yet troubled by life's complexities, simply wanting a cuddle or to look at a family photo album or to have a story read to them.

Family and friends at home and work walk alongside us too, lending support, offering encouragement and just being there. I'm not an island. And, just maybe, love really is all you need.

Certainly, in my professional life, I have seen endless and undeniable evidence of the staggering harm caused by the absence of love: in abusive homes, in traumatised childhoods, on violent streets and stairwells, in alienating neighbourhoods and divided communities, in the desperate lost lives of the lonely and the afraid. None of us is an island.

Then there is the height of life. Governments don't do God. Much of the watching world, me very much included, is sceptical about this thing called religion: fearful of extremism of every kind, cynical about motivation, appalled by hypocrisy.

But faith? The truth is, I am less certain of more things than I have ever been before. I have many more questions than I have answers. But I have begun to discover this thing called grace: the rumour that I am loved beyond measure, just as I am.

*

I stay working with Cress for the next six or seven months, slowly building up my hours and days. I go at a fraction of my old pace. She tasks me with the development of a series of four large-scale briefings for frontline officers and staff, providing input and insight into the police response to major terrorist incidents. Which leads me back to the power of stories. I decide that, rather than the usual chalk-and-talk approach to training, I want to find people who have stories to tell.

With the help of colleagues, I manage to find one of the survivors of 7/7 and the officer who helped save his life. We find a Senior Investigating Officer from the Counter Terrorism Command. We find the Met PC who is a leading UK authority on explosives and bomb making. We find a convicted terrorist who has had a fundamental change of mind and heart and who now supports police investigations. We find a number of the officers who responded to the murder of Lee Rigby, including those who were first on scene. I still find it almost impossible to look at the photos and CCTV footage of what happened in Woolwich that day, but as the most recent successful terrorist attack in London, it needs to feature as part of the briefings.

Having found this collection of remarkable people, I simply let them tell their tales, on film and on a platform in front of hundreds of cops and their colleagues. They speak of astounding courage and powerful humanity, of horror and heartbreak and rescue and redemption in circumstances that played out beyond the view and imagination of most ordinary people. They tell of just how extraordinary human beings can be.

When the survivor and the former terrorist greet one another on stage with smiles and a warm handshake, you can't take your eyes off them. It presents a remarkable image of forgiveness and healing. The feedback we receive following the briefings is stunning, with significant numbers suggesting that it was the best police training event they have ever attended. Stories matter, you see.

*

It's a Saturday afternoon in July 2014 and I'm chatting on the phone to Dad. Twelve weeks ago, he was given a terminal diagnosis, with six to twelve months to live. The cancer has spread to his lymph nodes and his body is failing him.

He's lying on the sofa at Mum's place, watching the cricket. Like son, like father. Last night he was sick in the bath and, this morning, he woke up feeling confused. Neither of those things has happened before. But he seems more or less OK now – it's still Dad on the other end of the line, talking with chuckling pessimism about England's chances against the Aussies. I tell him to take it easy, to rest well.

It's the last time I ever hear his voice.

*

The following day is Jessie's tenth birthday and we wake up to that air of joyful anticipation, a set of smiling faces appearing round the bedroom door and the sound of wrapping paper being torn as the girls all clamber up onto our bed. The best of times.

There's a loud knock on the front door. Bit early for deliveries. I wander down the stairs in my dressing gown – the chatter of happy voices drifting down with me.

It's Charlie, a close and longstanding family friend who lives just round the corner from us. He has a troubled look on his face and I feel a shudder in my soul. 'You need to call your mum.'

My mobile was switched off overnight and our landline isn't working. Mum was evidently trying to get hold of me and rang Charlie as a last resort.

'Has he died?'

'I don't think so, but you need to call home straight away.'

I woke up an hour ago, to a celebration of the wonders of my first child's birth. Now I'm standing hesitantly on my front doorstep, faced with the jarring possibility of my old man's death. Charlie hugs me and walks slowly away.

I don't want to upset the kids. I don't want to spoil the day. I don't want to burst the birthday balloon. I give Bear a whispered hint of what's happening and find a quiet corner of the house. I manage to get hold of my sister Annie on the phone. Dad was rushed into Basingstoke Hospital in the early hours of this morning. He's unconscious and may not make it to the end of the day. My heart fractures, caught between the living and the dying in London and Hampshire.

I hang on at home for the lunch party – a clamour of bubbly ten year olds drinking sparkling grape juice from plastic flutes. But my mind keeps straying down the A3 and to the gathering at Dad's side. I hug my girls and I hold Bear before I climb into the car, head and heart churning as I stretch a succession of speed limits. *Please God, can I get there in time.*

The pills I've been taking for the last year or so have taken the edge off my emotions and I just have no idea how I'm going to feel, how I'm going to react when I get there. I worry that I won't be able to cry when I know that I'm going to need to.

I find myself in the queue for the hospital car park behind Gerald, my brother-in-law. Turns out he's just been to the station to collect Father Owen. Owen is a parish priest from south-east London and one of Dad's dearest and oldest friends. He was Dad's best man when he and Mum got married almost fifty years ago. We smile a mournful smile, share an embrace and the three of us make our way up to the ward together.

There's Dad, oxygen mask on his face and nothing more than a bed sheet to cover his dignity. He's still with us. There's Mum and my two sisters, eyes reddening and arms reaching. One of my cousins and her husband are there too. Dad's sister and her husband and the hospital chaplain make up our small crowd.

For a while now, Mum and Dad have been talking about getting remarried. It represents one of the more unexpected endings, but he wants to meet his Maker reconciled to his wife. They just thought they had a little more time.

Dad can no longer speak, but we all know what he wanted and Joyce, his sister, is ready to do the talking for him. Father

Owen, dressed in the simple garments of priesthood, picks up an official-looking book. With another smile, he explains that there are two sorts of wedding: those in the eyes of the law and those in the eyes of God. 'Those in the eyes of the law require lots of paperwork; those in the eyes of God don't require any at all,' he says.

He opens the book and begins. As I perch on the arm of a hospital chair, a hastily sourced rose pinned to my T-shirt, I watch my mum and dad get married for the second time. And the tears fall.

*

I sit staring at the naked bridegroom, as my sister Mary has now christened him, and there is a simple perfection and a perfect simplicity to it all – a picture of extraordinary restoration. To borrow from T. S. Eliot, 'Dad has reached the end of all his exploring' and, as we pose for a series of entirely unconventional wedding snaps, I fully expect him to slip away. But he breathes quietly on.

I decide to stay down at Mum's place and see what the night brings. Bear and the girls understand. Dad breathes on for seven more days. Joyce later suggests that he must have been determined to stick around for the honeymoon.

*

Tuesday evening comes and I'm sitting at Dad's bedside with Mum and my sisters, getting ready to say another sad good-bye (how many of those have there been in the last thirty years?), when I have an unavoidable sense that I just need to spend some time alone with him. I ask the others if they mind. We're on a busy ward, but the curtain is drawn round us, offering a certain amount of privacy.

I start to talk to him in whispered tones. I tell him all the things I need to say and I speak for him too. I tell him that I know he's sorry for the pain of the past. I tell him that I know he's proud of me. I tell him that I know he loves me. And he breathes quietly on.

*

Dad dies the following Sunday and I am there to kiss his forehead. At his funeral a couple of weeks later, I preach his last sermon for him. He had prepared it a couple of days before that final ambulance ride and it had remained, unspoken, on his desk at home. It is a three-minute meditation on the Parable of the Sower, a short story from the Gospels, and it is my great privilege to give it voice. He has found peace at last. On this long road back from serious illness, I am finding some too.

*

While there is nothing on God's earth that would tempt me to repeat the descent into darkness – if indeed that choice is mine to make – neither is there anything that would persuade me to forfeit the experience of the last few years and all that I continue to learn along the way. Life might, of necessity, be slower these days, but it is also, somehow, deeper, richer and kinder. And I will never regret all my years as a police officer. Quite the opposite in fact. If I had my time over again, I would do it all again. I might go about it a little differently of course, but I would still choose to be a boy in blue. From that first moment as a teenager on Hammersmith Broadway until now, this extraordinary job has captivated me.

Policing is an affair of the heart and the soul, an imperfect response to an imperfect world. It matters more than I can say. But I am learning to accept that there are some things I just can't do any more – that there are some things that are just not good for me. I can no longer do exhaustion: endless long hours over extended periods of time, the unique and punishing demands of shift working and the expectation that I take my share of on-call responsibilities. These are the things I used to thrive on. The countless hours were just part of the job, nights were my favourite time to be at work and an off-duty phone call was a thing to relish.

But I'm not quite the man I used to be. I can no longer do stress: unmanageable workloads, unworkable deadlines, unreasonable expectations. I just don't have the gas in the tank. And I can no longer do trauma.

It was different when I was younger, before I was ill. When I was fourteen or fifteen, a lad from my school was knocked off his bike and killed. I remember the news coming through. The following morning, I saw another boy who had been there when it happened. I ran straight up to him. My first, insensitive, thought was that I wanted to know the story. It was the same compulsion that had pulled me towards the lifeboat on Little Haven beach all those years before. Somehow, I was drawn towards the sadness.

Later, as part of my application to join the Met, I attended an assessment centre at Sussex Police HQ. At the end of the second day, a group of us were left alone in a room filled with piles of old crime-scene pictures and encouraged to sift our way through them. What we saw were images of horror beyond darkest imaginings. I pored over them, fascinated.

When I finally joined, I wanted to be at every scene, to be where the action was, where the grim realities were to be found. I didn't hesitate, I just plunged straight in. As time passed and I became more senior, I wanted to set the example, to be where my officers were, doing what they were doing. Never ask someone to do something that you're not prepared to do yourself. But there came a time when I had seen enough. I couldn't tell you exactly when it was. I suspect it happened over time. The slow drip, drip.

All I know is that I have seen enough now. Were that not the case, I would still be impatient to get back to operational policing. There is so much that I miss. The banter of the parade room, the camaraderie that is shared uniquely among frontline cops. The adrenalin and the sense of urgency. The thrill of the chase. The headlong rush of blues and twos and the sheer breathlessness of it all. I miss the voice at the other end of the phone asking that simple question, 'Are you ready to save a life?' I miss the dull thud as the door goes in on the drug dealer's flat, the urgent and repeated shouts of 'police' as we scramble through the door. I miss being able to do things without thinking, without needing to ask whether I have the strength – physically, emotionally or psychologically – to do what needs to be done. What I don't miss is the tiredness, the heartbreak and the strain. But, here's a thing. My experiences are by no means unusual. I've worked with police officers who have seen many more dead bodies than me, who have been to many more fatal accidents than me, who have been injured far more severely than me, who have been faced with the unthinkable on many more occasions than I have. Sometimes I wonder how they manage to keep going. Perhaps they're just stronger than me. Perhaps they're holding it together better than I ever could. Perhaps they don't suffer in the same ways that I have. Some people get sick, some people don't. That's just the way of things. But perhaps some of them are hurting too. We all have our stories and we all have our scars.

*

I am a PC at the scene of a domestic stabbing, chaos and bandages and grief scattered all around me.

I am a sergeant in south London delivering the news that no one wants to hear.

I am an inspector at the scene of a shooting in west London. The victim is lying, fighting for breath, on the ground in front of me.

I am a duty officer taking a vulnerable child into police protection.

I am a nervous groom, standing at the front of the church, waiting for my bride.

I am a chief inspector delivering a briefing on the morning after the suicide bombers struck.

I am a dad, cradling my newborn daughter in my arms.

I am a hostage negotiator talking to a man and pleading with him to put the meat cleaver down.

I am a superintendent, sitting silently in a north London church as the coffin of an innocent young man is carried in.

I am a chief superintendent in the custody suite at Peckham, watching the PC watching the prisoner who has been put on suicide watch.

I am a Borough Commander standing on the Thames towpath, talking to a bandaged teenager who was stabbed earlier in the week and who doesn't seem to give a damn.

I am a middle-aged man, once broken almost beyond repair. Slowly mending.

Still believing in hope.

Epilogue

Almost five years since I fell. More than twenty-five years since I joined. Just a couple of weeks before I retire.

I'm sitting at my kitchen table, under the glass roof and the morning light, with my battered old warrant card lying open in front of me. The writing on it tells me that I am a police officer and that it represents my *'authority for executing the duties'* of a constable. It bears the signature of the Commissioner of Police of the Metropolis. Alongside a scuffed headshot of a younger me, you can still make out the Met's crest and the unique warrant number – 193053 – allocated to me as a Training School recruit in 1992. It's the number I have carried with me every day of my policing life.

But there's more to my warrant card than the simple words and images it displays. There are other, deeper stories behind it. Stories of identity and belonging: of who I am and have been – and of the great big, glorious, dysfunctional family

275

that I have been a part of ever since I started out on this adventure. Stories of authority and responsibility, of duty and service, of those who have gone before and of my small part in a history that reaches all the way back to 1829, when the Metropolitan Police was founded.

Then there are the memories it prompts: of my first day on patrol and my first vehicle stop; of catching my reflection in tall shop windows and an unmistakeable sense of pride at what – and who – I saw there; of my first arrest, my first dead body, my first car crash, my first pub fight, my first murder scene; of laughter and tears, exhaustion and elation, heartbreak and hope.

And every contact left a trace.

In just a handful of days' time, I will have to hand my warrant card back. The normal span of a policing lifetime is thirty years – so retirement comes four and a half years earlier than it was supposed to. I'm going on the grounds of ill health. I made it back to work, but I never made it back to full duties. I'm a whole lot better than I was, but some of the damage is permanent: the inability to deal with trauma; the inability to deal with strain; the exhaustion that continues to overtake me with frustrating regularity.

I still love the job and the people who do it. I love them with all my heart and soul. But my days of blue lighting and hostage negotiating, siege commanding and door kicking, foot chasing and thief nicking are now done.

*

For the first three years after falling ill, I made steady progress in my recovery. I built up my hours and my workload – gently, carefully, watching constantly for any sign that all might not be well. I remained a long way short of my capacity and capability as a Borough Commander, but I was improving.

I began to regain a little of my old confidence and resilience – and I started to dream police dreams again. Maybe I would make it back to operational duties after all. I even began to think about the possibility of applying for promotion in the future.

Cress had moved on to another post and I found myself working for the Met's Director of HR, making myself useful wherever I could. At the start of 2016, she and I agreed that I was ready to step up my recovery. I still wasn't fully mended, but I was well enough to take on a proper job. So I was given a programme-director role in officer recruitment and training. It was the first time in three years that I had had direct responsibility for anyone other than myself – a small, dedicated team of officers and staff with plenty of work to be done. I was travelling on the Tube every day, with a full schedule of meetings and the inevitable pressure to deliver.

And I lasted no more than six weeks before I started to feel very seriously ill. The tiredness returned and deepened. The anxiety intensified. And the storm began to gather once more. I could feel my feet slipping all over again.

But this time I asked for help. Thank God I did.

*

The author Matt Haig has suggested that depression is 90 per cent mystery – and I reckon that number is about right.

I don't fully understand what happened to me in April 2013, and I don't fully understand what happened to me in

June 2016. But the available expertise would seem to suggest that people who have experienced one episode of depressive illness are more vulnerable to it happening again.

Perhaps that's me. Perhaps I am always going to need to live my life a little more carefully than others. I certainly know that there will be more days when I need to put my hand up and ask for help. The alternative is to fall back into darkness.

Asking for that help in 2016 meant that I was off work for weeks rather than months and that the worst of the weather passed overhead relatively quickly. But it also meant a swift end to the new role I had taken on and the beginnings of some tough conversations.

At the start of the year, Bear and I had taken out a five-year fixed mortgage, timed to finish just before my anticipated retirement date. I was still planning – wanting – to see out every one of my thirty years.

But, just a handful of months later, I was talking with colleagues about the possibility of an early departure because of my illness. I went back to see the Met's Consultant Psychiatrist – a kind man who had supported me throughout the previous three years. Not knowing what had happened to me, he was expecting to report on the next stage of my recovery. Instead, he was faced by a person deeply shaken by the latest realisation of his fragile state and entirely uncertain about what the future might hold. He listened and he was wise. He told me that life was supposed to be about more than just getting by. As he spoke, I realised that, without knowing it, I had been playing a game of brinkmanship with my health – seeing how close I could get to the edge without actually stumbling over it. And that's no way to live.

So, in September 2016, my boss filled out a form recommending me for ill-health retirement (IHR) from the Met. The paperwork stated that, in her view, I was no longer fit to perform the duties of a police officer and that my limitations were likely to be permanent. Her opinion was endorsed by the psychiatrist and by the Met's Chief Medical Officer.

No longer fit to perform the duties of a police officer.

That's a heck of a thing to be told. Even if you know it to be true. Because this is all I ever wanted to do – all I ever wanted to be. Until life happened.

The IHR process took more than 18 months to run its course. And it was horrible. My colleagues were, as ever, wonderful, but the process itself was devoid of any form of humanity. It should never be that way.

*

All the while, I continued to write.

I found an agent. She found a publisher. And I signed a book deal.

It hadn't been part of any plan. All I had ever wanted was to be a police officer – and to go wherever that journey might take me. I had only started writing just before falling ill the first time round. I was so full of the memories of all I had seen and heard and done as a police officer that it was almost a compulsion – an essential means of relieving the pressure inside.

As I recovered at home later on, it became a way to get my brain working again. It became part of the recovery process. And then I found that I loved it.

In May 2017, I became a published author. And the telling of my story was a kind of coming out: the admissions of a man who broke and who struggles with his mental health. Because the stigma undoubtedly remains – not least because we tend to be afraid of the things we can't explain or don't understand. I discovered a particular kind of vulnerability: the inevitable consequence of giving away something of myself and of not knowing how people might respond. Was I going to be strong enough to cope with whatever came my way?

But the book launch was one of the happiest nights of my life, surrounded by family and friends and love and affirmation – and a long queue of smiling faces wanting me to sign their copy.

In the days and weeks and months that followed, kindness was never far away: letters and cards and texts and messages and colleagues stopping me in the Yard canteen to say that they had just finished the last chapter.

The coppers told me that my story could have been their story and they thanked me for telling it. And people from beyond policing told me that it had offered them a glimpse into a world previously beyond their knowing. It had left them with a new sense of appreciation and gratitude for those everyday heroes and heroines who police our communities.

In the meantime, for those police officers out patrolling the streets of the capital, the emergency calls just kept on coming.

*

In December 2017 London's Guildhall played host to a unique and very special gathering of police officers, emergency-services colleagues and members of the public. Welcomed jointly by the Met, British Transport Police and the City of London Police, they came to honour those who had responded to the succession of terrorist attacks that had happened in London earlier that year. And to remember those who had died.

Something like two hundred commendations were awarded at the ceremony, in recognition of the frankly staggering levels of heroism and humanity displayed following the attacks at Westminster Bridge, London Bridge and Finsbury Park. The stories behind each of them are breathtaking: in the face of the very worst that human beings are capable of, we were witnesses to the very, very best. Amongst the endless astonishing accounts, the stories of three men lingered with me the longest.

At about 2.40 p.m. on Wednesday 22 March 2017, a terrorist launched an attack on Westminster Bridge and at the Houses of Parliament. Five people were murdered and many more were injured.

Keith Palmer was a police officer, a husband and a dad. Unarmed, he stepped forwards – and he paid the greatest price of all.

I couldn't look at the pictures from the scene or watch the coverage on TV. I couldn't read the eyewitness accounts or even pick up a newspaper the following morning. It was all far more than I could bear. But, on a grey April morning, I took my place on the streets near Southwark Cathedral and I stood for Keith. Thousands of police officers lined the pavements and we bowed our heads as he made his last journey. The flowers on the front of the hearse spelt out *No. 1 Daddy* and I mourned a man I had never known. It was the very least I could do.

Just after 10 p.m. on Saturday 3 June 2017, alongside that same cathedral, three terrorists carried out an attack on London Bridge and at Borough Market. Eight people were murdered and forty-eight more were rushed to hospital. The attackers were armed with knives and wearing what appeared to be suicide vests.

Again, I was unable even to look. But I heard about the actions of two of my colleagues. Wayne Marques is a British Transport Police officer. He had just started his shift at London Bridge when the attack happened. And he didn't hesitate. Armed only with his baton, he ran to confront the terrorists. He suffered major injuries to his head, left hand and left leg.

Charlie Guenigault is a Metropolitan Police officer from my old borough, Southwark. He was off duty with friends, enjoying a drink near London Bridge when the attack happened. And he didn't hesitate. Armed with nothing more than an overwhelming sense of duty, he ran to help PC Marques. He was stabbed in his head, leg, back and stomach. He needed surgery to remove his spleen.

And I find that I begin to run out of words to describe how I feel about what they did that night – and about what Keith did just a few weeks before. These men are giants, and theirs are stories for the ages. As are those of each one of their colleagues – and of the medical staff and members of the public who played their various parts with absolute distinction. They represent the very finest of who we are and what we can be.

To borrow from remarks made at the commendation ceremony by Helen Ball, one of the Met's Assistant Commissioners, words cannot replace what we have lost – and we would not seek for them to do so. So we will simply tell the stories of those who were there.

And still the 999 calls keep coming.

These are now the most challenging times for policing in Britain since the end of the Second World War. That isn't exaggeration for effect; it's just a simple statement of fact.

Crime is rising, particularly crime of the most serious kinds. Demand on policing is rising, not least as a consequence of the undeniable cracks that have appeared in the provision of other frontline public services. Complexity is rising as crime crosses geographic borders and technological frontiers. Risk and threat are rising as officers and staff remain explicit terrorist targets. And, whilst all of this is happening, the UK population is rising – by close to five million in the last ten years alone.

But, at the same time, police resources and budgets are falling significantly. Police officer numbers in England and Wales have dropped by more than 21,000 since 2010 and now sit at the lowest levels since comparable records began. And there remains a pressing demand for further cuts.

The reality is unavoidably troubling. But most troubling of

all is the very personal impact all this is having on individual police officers and staff who are stumbling under the loads they are carrying. Hearts remain willing but, in too many cases now, minds and bodies are breaking.

We need to listen to the accounts being given by those on the policing frontline. Then we need to understand that there is a difference between listening and hearing – and between hearing and actually doing something about what's being said.

As I look around me in the Met and beyond, I see some of the finest women and men you could ever hope to meet, working under far greater pressure and strain than I have ever known. The very least they deserve is the very best support we can give them.

*

As for me, I am going to go a little more slowly and gently than before – out of both necessity and choice.

In one of my quieter moments, for reasons that aren't immediately obvious, I find myself thinking about those dull pre-flight safety briefings you are obliged to sit through on aeroplanes. In particular, I think about the part that describes the oxygen masks dropping down from the ceiling of the plane. Even if I have my youngest daughter sitting next to me, the instruction is clear: I am to fit my own mask before I make any attempt to fit hers. Because my capacity to look after her depends on my capacity to look after myself. I am of no use to her whatsoever if I can't breathe.

As it is on aeroplanes, so it is in life – and most certainly in policing. I love that old quote attributed to American TV presenter Fred Rogers:

When I was a boy and I would see scary things in the news, my mother would say to me, 'Look for the helpers. You will always find people who are helping.' To this day, especially in times of disaster, I remember my mother's words, and I am always comforted by realising that there are still so many helpers — so many caring people in this world.

Before they are anything else, police officers are helpers. Especially in times of disaster. But it turns out that our ability to look after anyone else is inextricably connected to our ability to look after ourselves. It has taken me the best part of forty-eight years and a massive nervous breakdown to learn that.

These days, I go to bed a little earlier and I sleep a little longer than I used to. In the mornings I walk Puffin, the family's two-year-old spaniel who thinks he's one of the children and doesn't understand that he really isn't supposed to curl up on our bed. I take time and space to think and breathe and say my prayers. I select the books I read and the films I watch carefully, avoiding anything that might upset or traumatise. I look for tales of hope and redemption, for stories that end well.

Life didn't quite work out as planned, but there remains so much to be grateful for: the extraordinary love of my wife; the hours and days spent with our three beautiful girls; the faithfulness of friends and the kindness of those I barely know; learning how to rest in a world that is moving far too fast; the discovery of writing and of the healing to be found in the telling of tales; the opportunity to stand up and speak up for the things that have to matter more; the discovery of that thing called grace.

*

Two weeks from now, I will put my warrant card in my trouser pocket for the last time. Then I will take the Tube to Scotland Yard and hand it back in. It was mine for more than a quarter of a century and it was the greatest privilege of my working life to serve.

I love this extraordinary job. I love the extraordinary men and women who do it. And I will always feel pride of the finest kind.

Because I was a boy in blue.

Acknowledgements

Saying thank you matters. And there are a lot of people to thank. My endless gratitude and appreciation goes to:

Those kind souls who have cheered me on, who volunteered to read earlier drafts of the book, and who offered all sorts of advice and encouragement along the way. In particular, Lynne Owens, Tom Benyon, Katie Levell, Dr Annie Sutherland, Mary Taylor, Steve Kavanagh, Charlie Cumming, Jamie Owen, Patrick Regan, Clare Davies, Gareth Edwards, Xandra Bingley and Anna Purser.

My agent, the wonderful Laura Williams at PFD, who believed in this book and who improved it in any number of ways.

Ben Perkins, who introduced me to Laura.

Paul Murphy, Helen Richardson, Sarah Benton and the rest of the remarkable team at Weidenfeld & Nicolson. I am honoured beyond words to carry your name on this book.

Those extraordinary friends who walked with me through the darkest days. In particular, Mark, Tom, John,

Patrick, Jonathan, Charlie, Ush, Woody, Steph, Jane, Matt and Richard.

My friends and colleagues from the Police Superintendents' Association of England and Wales.

The bosses who understand that people matter. In particular, Kav, Cress, Lynne, Clare and Craig.

The boys and girls in blue who I have served alongside for so many years. Your courage and compassion are without equal.

Jessie, Charlie and Emily – my glorious girls.

And to Bear – the best thing that ever happened to me. This book is for you.